feathers
that fly

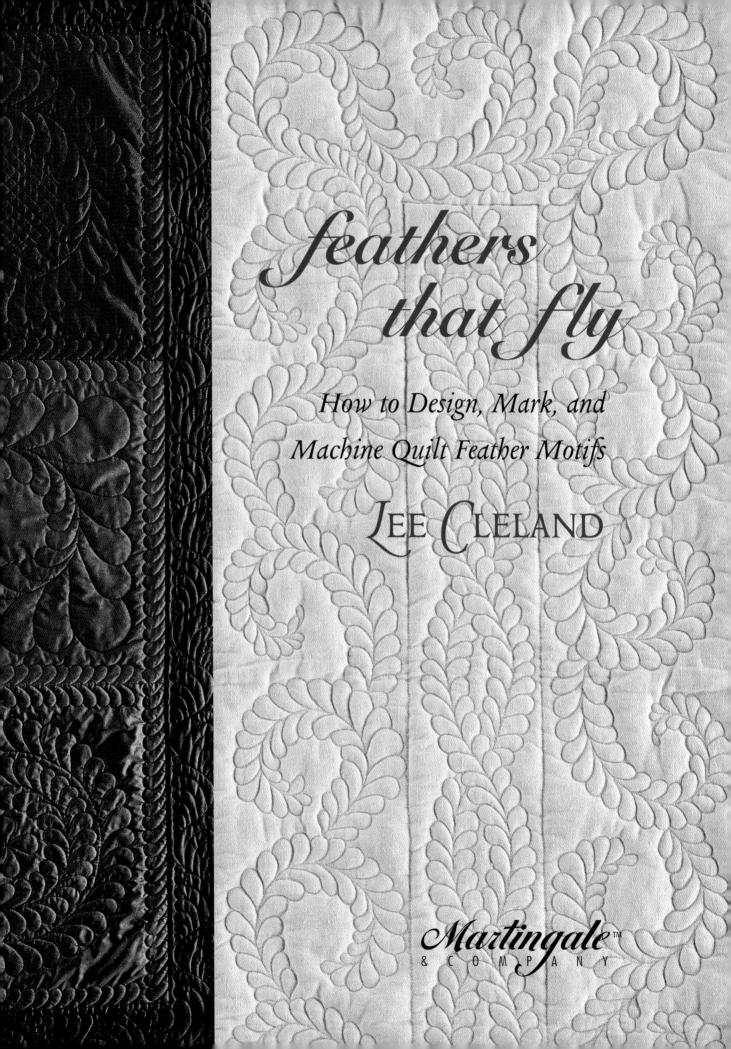

feathers that fly

How to Design, Mark, and Machine Quilt Feather Motifs

Lee Cleland

Martingale™
& COMPANY

Feathers That Fly: How to Design, Mark, and Machine Quilt Feather Motifs
© 2002 by Lee Cleland

Martingale & Company
20205 144th Avenue NE
Woodinville, WA 98072-8478
www.martingale-pub.com

Credits

President ~ Nancy J. Martin
CEO ~ Daniel J. Martin
Publisher ~ Jane Hamada
Editorial Director ~ Mary V. Green
Managing Editor ~ Tina Cook
Technical Editor ~ Barbara Weiland
Copy Editor ~ Karen Koll
Design Director ~ Stan Green
Illustrator ~ Laurel Strand
Cover and Text Designer ~ Stan Green
Photographers ~ Andy Payne and Oliver Ford of Photographix, Sydney, Australia

Printed in China
07 06 05 04 03 02   8 7 6 5 4 3 2 1

Library of Congress Cataloging-in-Publication Data

Cleland, Lee.
    Feathers that fly : how to design, mark, and machine quilt feather motifs /
Lee Cleland.
        p. cm.
    ISBN 1-56477-455-4
    1. Machine quilting—Patterns. 2. Patchwork—Patterns. I. Title.
    TT835 .C5945 2002
    746.46'041—dc21
                                                                    2002011800

Mission Statement

We are dedicated to providing quality products and service by working together to inspire creativity and to enrich the lives we touch.

4

Contents

An idea takes wing

In 1990, I made a pieced navy-and-white feathered star quilt that went on to win "Best of Show" at the Quilters' Guild Exhibition in Sydney, Australia. Machine pieced and quilted, my award-winning quilt had been a source of frustration during its making. Finding feathered quilting designs that fit the areas I wished to quilt proved next to impossible. I finally located three designs that fit the spaces in my quilt, but my design search taught me how little I really knew about quilting designs in general and feather designs in particular. It led me on a new search for information on how to design quilting patterns—particularly on how to create feathered quilting designs.

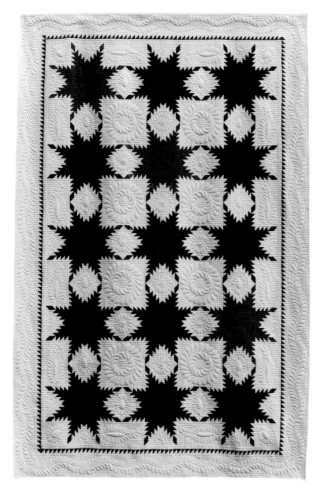

BLUE FEATHERED STARS I
68" x 104"
My exploration of feathered quilting designs began with this quilt, which won "Best of Show" at The Quilters' Guild Inc. Exhibition in Sydney, Australia in 1990.
Photo by Lee Cleland.

Fine Feathers, a book by Marianne Fons, proved to be a helpful resource, but all of the work shown was hand quilted. Since I have been an avid machine quilter since 1968, it seemed obvious that a book on developing and using feathered patterns for machine quilting was a natural next step. More than a decade since my search for feathered patterns began, I am ready to share what I've learned with others who appreciate the elegance and beauty of feathered quilting designs. I hope this book will inspire you to try your hand at designing and stitching feathered quilting patterns on your machine.

Learning how to design your own feathers is freeing and great fun. I am one of those people who writes lists, likes precision, and tries to be organized—structured is another way to describe me—and yet, I've been able to create my own quilting designs that complement my pieced and whole-cloth quilts. So, even if you think you are not "creative enough" to design feathered quilting patterns, I know you can do it with my help.

Creating your own quilting patterns is not as difficult as you might think, once you know a few basic techniques and general principles. Turning corners with any quilting design can be challenging. Studying old quilts or appliqué designs is a good way to discover creative ways to solve a design problem.

The quilts in the "Gallery of Quilts" section of this book (beginning on page 122) will provide ideas on how to use feathered quilting designs in ways other than those discussed in the workbook section. Patterns for designs in these quilts are not included, but you will have the know-how to draft similar designs for your quilt, using the information in the text.

A number of the quilts in the gallery have won top prizes in major Australian quilt exhibitions, mostly for machine quilting. Because most of my quilts are made using fairly simple traditional pieced designs and plain fabrics, elaborate feathered quilting shows beautifully on their surfaces.

From simple to complex, traditional to contemporary, you will find a feathered quilting design in this book that suits your taste and your quilt—and you will learn how to draft it for a perfect fit. Enjoy the journey and just watch those "feathers fly" around and over the surface of your next quilt.

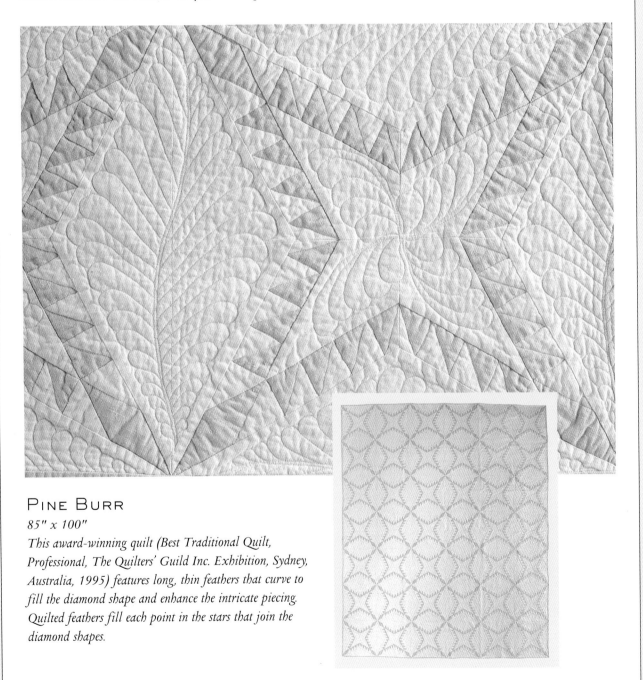

PINE BURR

85" x 100"

This award-winning quilt (Best Traditional Quilt, Professional, The Quilters' Guild Inc. Exhibition, Sydney, Australia, 1995) features long, thin feathers that curve to fill the diamond shape and enhance the intricate piecing. Quilted feathers fill each point in the stars that join the diamond shapes.

Getting started

Feathers that Fly is organized as a workbook. By following the step-by-step progression in the pages that follow, you will learn how to draw your own feathered quilting designs to fit any shape or border and how to turn corners with your designs so that they form a continuous pattern. (If you are a quilting teacher, you will find this a helpful resource to recommend to your students.)

On the other hand, if you prefer to use this book simply to make the quilts as shown, rather than learn to create your own feathered quilting patterns, instructions and quilting designs are included for that purpose.

In each chapter, you will follow step-by-step directions that guide you through the process of drawing traditional feathers. You will begin with the simplest feathers to draw, and you will progress to the more difficult shapes, including contemporary feather designs, as you gain skill and confidence. Every chapter includes drawing exercises, and most include practice projects so that you can work on something small while you perfect your feather drawing and stitching skills. The final project is one that draws on designs from throughout the book, providing you with the opportunity to finish a larger project while you continue to refine your skills. The gallery quilts provide additional design application and inspiration.

Although this is a workbook, I suggest you trace the designs and working samples from the book onto separate sheets of paper for your practice design sessions to keep your book clean for permanent reference.

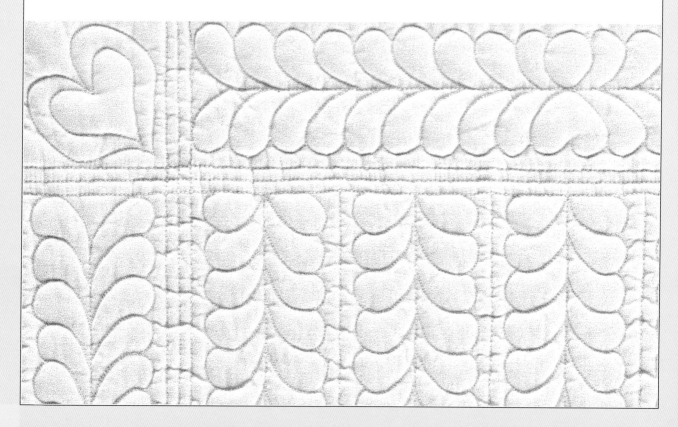

Hopefully, using this book to create feathered quilting designs will be the catalyst for your own creative journey with quilting designs. Feel free to use the designs and instructions provided to create your own feather designs and design combinations to enhance your quilts.

Gathering Your Supplies

You will need only a few simple supplies to learn how to draw elegant feather designs:

Calculator

Coin. The size should match as closely as possible the sizes shown here.

Dark-Colored Permanent Marking Pen. The most common brands are Sharpie in America and Texta in Australia.

Drawing Compass. This should have an extension arm.

Eraser

Lead Pencils

Long Measuring Tape

Rotary Cutting Ruler. The 6" x 24" size is best.

Small (12") Ruler. This should be marked in sixteenths of an inch.

Tracing Paper. In Australia, I can get a roll of 10"-wide inexpensive "greaseproof paper" from the supermarket. Freezer paper is the closest inexpensive American substitute, but I find it too thick, so I recommend buying a supply of tracing paper for the design exercises.

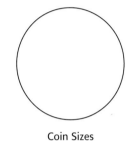

Coin Sizes

Enlarging the Designs

Many of the quilting patterns included in this book are designed to fit 15" squares. To enlarge them, you will need to use a photocopier. With each design, you will find a percentage that indicates how much to enlarge it to bring it up to the correct size. If the percentage is 200 percent, you must double the size (actual size is 100 percent). However, some photocopiers only enlarge up to 150 percent. In that case, you would first enlarge it by 150 percent and then enlarge the result by 133 percent to get a total enlargement of 200 percent. It may be necessary to make the photocopy in two or three sections and tape them together to complete the design.

CHAPTER 1

Straight-spine feathered quilting designs

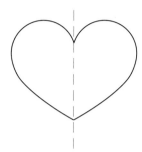

Drawing traditional feathers is easy. Think about it. A feather is really just half of a simple heart shape. You don't need a fancifully shaped heart or a folk-art heart for these designs. If you draw half a heart, you have one feather. However, feathers are never quilted by themselves but rather in combination to create other designs.

Feather-Drawing Guidelines

There are three basic guidelines to follow as you work through the exercises in this book while you learn to draw and stitch beautiful feathered quilting designs.

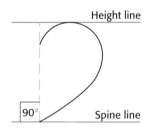

1. To draw a feather, you must begin with 2 parallel lines spaced as far apart as the desired height of your finished feathers. One of these lines is called the spine and the other is the height line. The top or curved part of the feather begins at the height line. The bottom of the half heart (feather) sits or finishes at the spine line.

2. The half heart should finish at the spine line, directly in line with where it starts. The imaginary line connecting the upper curve and the lower end of the feather is perpendicular to the spine.

3. Begin drawing each new half-heart shape (feather) *from the top down* in one movement or "swoop." These feathers appear to overlap each other, with the first feather you draw appearing to be the feather on top of all the others. Drawing feathers in this manner (rather than from the bottom up) will help train your hand and eyes to work in concert so that you will be able to draw beautiful free-hand feathers as you gain experience. This is also the machine-stitching direction you will follow when you quilt feathered designs; drawing them in the same direction you will be stitching actually helps you stitch more accurately. It's all a matter of developing eye, hand, and stitching coordination so that the quilting motion becomes second nature to you.

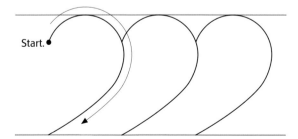

Drawing Your First Straight-Spine Feathers

Are you ready to draw your first feathers? Get out your supplies (see page 9).

Exercise 1: Just Tracing

1. On a clean sheet of paper, trace the design below. Draw the 2 parallel lines (the spine and the height line) and carefully trace the feathers. Begin with the feather marked 1 and always start tracing at the top of the curve for each feather, continuing down and around the curve to the spine line.

2. Draw the second feather, starting at the top where it touches the outside curve of the first feather. Follow the same path, around the curve and down to the spine line.

3. Continue across the row, tracing half-heart feathers in the same manner.

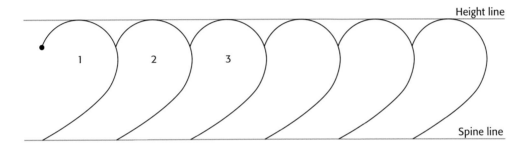

Exercise 2: The Coin Trick

As a beginner, you will probably find it difficult to keep the width at the top of the feathers consistent throughout. That's where a coin comes in handy. Use it as a template for drawing feather tops of the same width along the height line. I never use more than half of the coin top, and generally the top third is about right. The drawn coin tops should just touch each other along the height line.

1. Draw the spine and height line as directed above, but do not trace the feathers.

2. Use a small coin to draw 15 to 20 coin tops along the height line; then go back and start drawing the feathers as half hearts, drawing over the coin tops again so that you are training your mind and hand to learn how to draw feathers freehand (eventually).

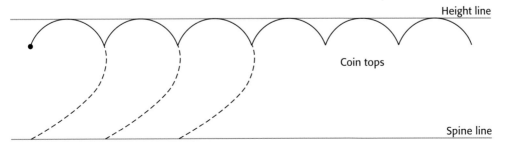

Some quilters find that putting a mark on the spine line directly below the start of the feather gives them a spot to aim for while they are drawing the feather. This mark (just a dot) would be on an imaginary line perpendicular to the spine from the beginning of the coin top. Do this exercise a couple of times and you'll start to get a feel for the shape of the feathers.

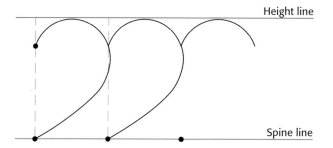

Drawing on Both Sides of the Spine

When you are comfortable drawing a line of single feathers, it's time to progress to drawing on both sides of the spine line—that's how most feather designs are drawn and quilted.

Exercise 1: Just Tracing

1. Trace the spine line and 2 height lines, one on each side of the spine and equidistant from it.

2. Trace the feathers, beginning with the first feather above the spine.

NOTE: Here's a place where you can apply the old adage, "Rules are made to be broken." Or, at least you can bend the rule a bit, to create a more fluid design.

When drawing the second line of feathers, note that they will look more fluid if the bottoms don't quite match up. Don't obsess about it, though. If a few

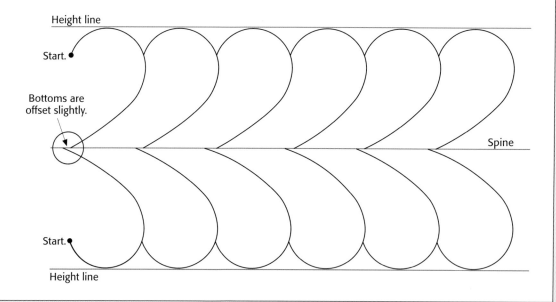

feathers touch, it does not matter. If the bottom of a feather touches the spine at the same place as a feather from the line above, offset the bottom of the feather slightly.

Exercise 2: On Your Own

1. Now draw or trace the spine and a height line on each side of it.

2. Using a small coin, draw the tops of the feathers.

3. Complete all the feathers yourself. I draw all the coin tops first and then go back and make the feathers, remembering to draw over the coin tops and then down to the spine line.

Repeat this exercise several times on clean sheets of paper. In the beginning, most quilters feel a little awkward drawing the feathers in one of the directions. Once you get used to the drawing movements required, your feathers will take shape more easily.

Taking a few minutes to analyze your work before you start the next practice sheet will also help you improve your technique. To analyze your work and set a course of correction, be sure to read through "Avoiding Pitfalls" on page 14.

Remember: We each have our own style. Your feathers do not have to be carbon copies of mine. Instead, strive for feathers that flow in a smooth curve from the beginning of the coin top until they touch the spine line.

Drawing Hearts and Teardrops

The straight-spine feather is a very useful design for filling sashing strips and wider borders, as illustrated in "Old English Tulips III" on page 126. However, with a few simple changes, this basic design takes on even more character. Since it requires two feathers, one a mirror image of the other, to make a full heart, you can use a heart shape at the center of a straight spine and draw the feathers out from the center on each side of the heart.

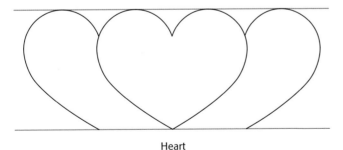

Heart

AVOIDING PITFALLS

It's only natural that the feathers you draw will take on their own special characteristics—each of us is unique. However, if your feathers go too far astray, you can correct your work. Read through the following feather descriptions and examine the illustrations to identify the drawing problem you are experiencing. Follow the guidelines for drawing feathers with better shapes.

- **FEATHERS THAT DON'T LOOK LIKE FEATHERS**

Check the shape you are actually drawing. It must be a half-heart shape, with the start and the finish of the feather in line, perpendicular to the spine.

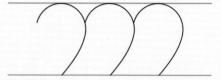

Feathers That Don't Look Like Feathers

- **STIFF FEATHERS**

Make sure the drawn line continues the curve of the "coin top." If it drops straight off the back of the coin top as shown, you lose the curve.

Stiff Feathers

- **BACKWARD-CURVING FEATHERS**

Examine the "style" of the half heart you are actually drawing. Drawing folk art–style half hearts makes feathers curve backward where they touch the spine. The result is a messy look with too many curves competing with each other for attention. Keep the heart shape simple for fluid feathers.

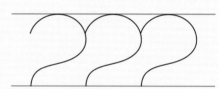

Backward-Curving Feathers

- **FLAT, LAZY FEATHERS**

If the curve you draw is too large, the feather will look like it's lying down along the spine line. "Lazy feathers" are far more difficult to quilt by machine. Strive for feathers that are softly curved to avoid the lazy-feather syndrome.

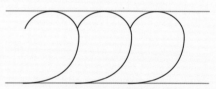

Flat, Lazy Feathers

- **S CURVES ALONG THE SPINE**

When you draw feathers on both sides of a spine line, they must be drawn from the same end of the spine and head in the same direction. If you have Ss, you have started the feathers from opposite ends of the spine line

In all cases, when correcting your feather-drawing style, think fatter but not so fat that your feathers decide to lie down and take a nap. Think voluptuous; think curved.

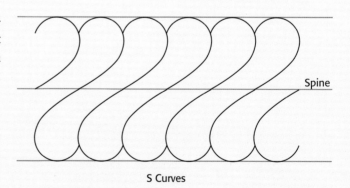

Spine

S Curves

The teardrop shape is a similar shape to the feather and can be used in the same way as a heart.

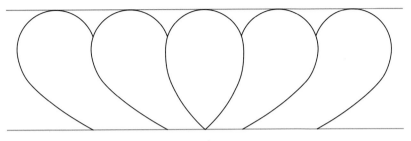

Teardrop

Hearts and teardrops are very useful for turning corners and in blocks where you want a quilting design to radiate from a point or to turn on an angle. I call these two motifs "turning points" for that reason. For now, we'll draw these shapes on a straight line, centering them on the spine between two height lines.

Exercise 1: Hearts and Teardrops

1. Trace the spine line and 2 height lines, the heart, and the teardrop.

2. Trace the feathers on one side of the spine. Start from the heart and draw out to the right and then to the left.

3. Trace the feathers on the other side of the spine. Start from the teardrop and work out to the right and then to the left.

NOTE: Because the heart is so much wider than the teardrop, there should be no problem with the bottoms of the feathers touching at the spine line. Each line of feathers is complete in and of itself and bears no relationship to the line of feathers on the other side of the spine. Sometimes in a long line of feathers, the bottoms of the feathers may line up, but then you can simply offset them as described on page 12.

Work to draw pleasing
feather shapes, but
don't obsess about
them. You'll wear out
your eraser trying to
make them absolutely
perfect. If you like the
shape and flow of
what you've drawn,
move on. You have
three more opportuni-
ties to fine-tune any
imperfections in your
designs before the
quilt is actually fin-
ished. Here's the whole
design and quilting
process in a nutshell:

1. Draw the original
    feather design in
    pencil.

2. Go over the final
    design with a per-
    manent marker.

3. Transfer the design
    to your quilt top.

4. Quilt.

You can make minor
adjustments to the
design at each stage.

Exercise 2: On Your Own

1. Trace the spine and height lines, the heart, and the teardrop.

2. Draw your own feathers, again using a small coin top as your guide to
    draw the feather tops first. Always start from the heart or the teardrop
    shape and work out or away from these "turning points" as you add
    the feathers.

Planning for Design Breathing Space

Any open space or shape on your quilt is a candidate for a feathered design,
but it takes some planning to create a design that complements the space.
If you overfill the area, the design will look squashed and crowded. If the
design is too small for the space, it will look lost. This is where "breathing
space" comes into play—it is an important part of the overall design.
Allowing for breathing space also gives you a bit of latitude if all of the
squares or shapes in your quilt are not quite exactly the same size.

Most of the designs included in this book have a ¼" margin of
breathing space all around, but a space of up to 1" is fine. If you are planning to use the feather design in tandem with a background pattern—a
diamond grid or stipple quilting for example—you may want even more
breathing space around the design.

The easiest way to plan for breathing space is to draw a full-scale
replica of the shape you wish to fill, and then draw lines inside the shape
that are the desired width for the breathing space. For example, if the open
space in a setting block in my quilt were 12" square, I would draw a 12"
square on my tracing paper, and an 11½" square centered inside it, which
allows ¼" of space on each side of the square. I call this 11½" square the
design area.

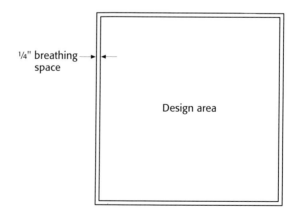

¼" breathing
space

Design area

Once the design area has been defined, it's time to fill the inner space with the desired quilting design. Draw the feathered design so that it just touches the line that defines the breathing space.

To design a feathered pattern for border corners, you have two options:

1. Treat the corner as a separate design area.

    Or

2. Create a continuous feather design that flows around the corners.

If you are treating each corner as a separate design area, follow the same procedure described above to set off the design area with at least ¼" of breathing space all around.

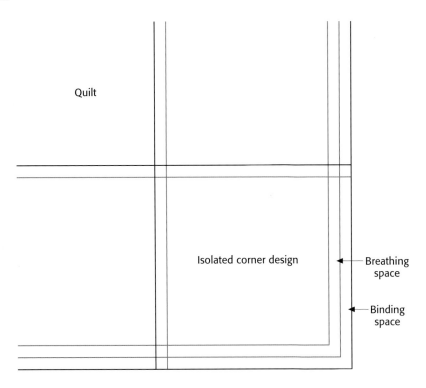

Quilt

Isolated corner design — Breathing space

— Binding space

For continuous border designs, you need breathing space only at the outer edge of the border and at the inside corner of each quilt corner. I also draw a line ¼" beyond the finished size of the project. When I am ready to complete the project with binding, I align the raw edge of the binding strip with this line and then stitch ¼" from the raw edge of the binding.

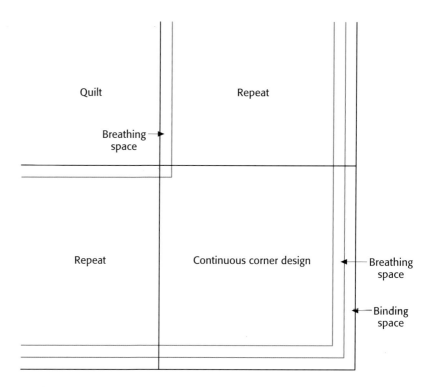

Do not draw the breathing space lines onto the quilt top. They are guidelines for the actual design and drawing process only. When my design is complete, I draw over the design lines on the tracing paper with a dark permanent marker. I do the same on the breathing-space lines and any piecing lines to help me position the design correctly within the designated space on the quilt top.

NOTE: When you are combining background fills such as stipple quilting, echo quilting, or grids with your feathered design, it is essential to quilt all the way to the piecing lines and edges of the quilt. This quilting does not end at breathing space lines.

Practice Project 1:
Straight-Spine Feathers Wall Hanging

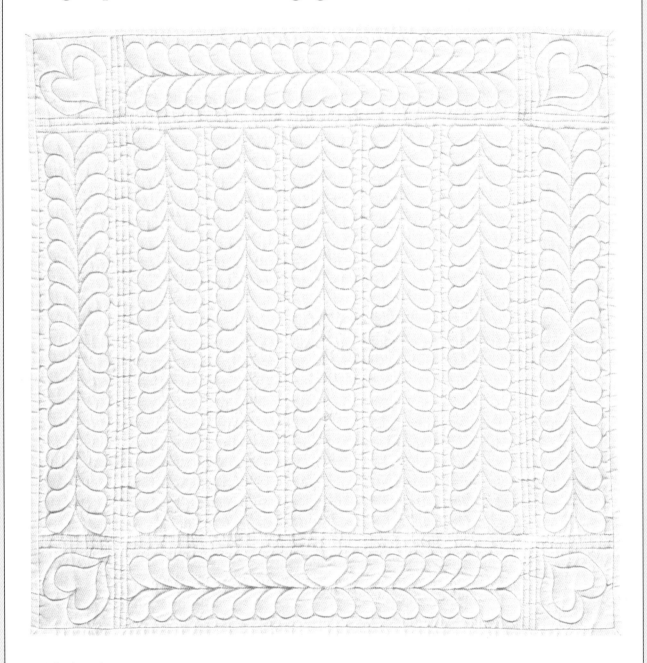

Finished Quilt Size: 22½" x 22½"

Row after row of straight-spine feather designs create a highly textured surface on this small quilt. Placing quilted hearts on point in each corner is an easy alternative to "turning the corner"—a good choice for beginners.

Simple rows of feathers work in tandem to make this striking wall hanging. It's a great practice project for drawing and quilting feathers. Use the designs provided or draw your own after working through the exercises below. Let the design illustrations be your guide.

Beautiful feathered quilting designs show up best on solid-colored fabrics. They tend to get lost on patterned fabrics.

Materials

Yardage is based on 42"-wide fabric, with 40" of usable width after preshrinking.

24" square of fabric for quilt top
26" square of fabric for backing
½ yd. fabric for binding and hanging sleeve
26" square of batting

Drawing the Feather Patterns

1. Trace design 1 (page 21) for the straight-spine feather to create a quilting pattern for your quilt. If you prefer to draw your own feather design, see "Note" below.

2. For the feather design with the heart and teardrop turning points, flip the design over and trace a mirror image to complete the design.

3. Go over both finished quilting patterns with a dark-colored permanent marker. Include the outline of the rectangle, the spine, and the lines for the breathing space.

NOTE: If you prefer to draw your own feather patterns, create the two feather designs to fit inside a 3" x 7½" rectangle. Remove ¼" from each long edge of the rectangle to create "breathing space" (see page 16). Use a small coin along the height lines to make feathers of a consistent width. When the rectangle is nearly full of feathers, finish with the last full feather that will fit. Don't try to squeeze just one more feather into the rectangle or the pattern will look crowded. For design 2, draw only half of the heart and teardrop and then feathers to fill the rest of this half design area. Both of these designs are only half the quilt top area and must be repeated (design 1) or flipped (design 2) to fill the area.

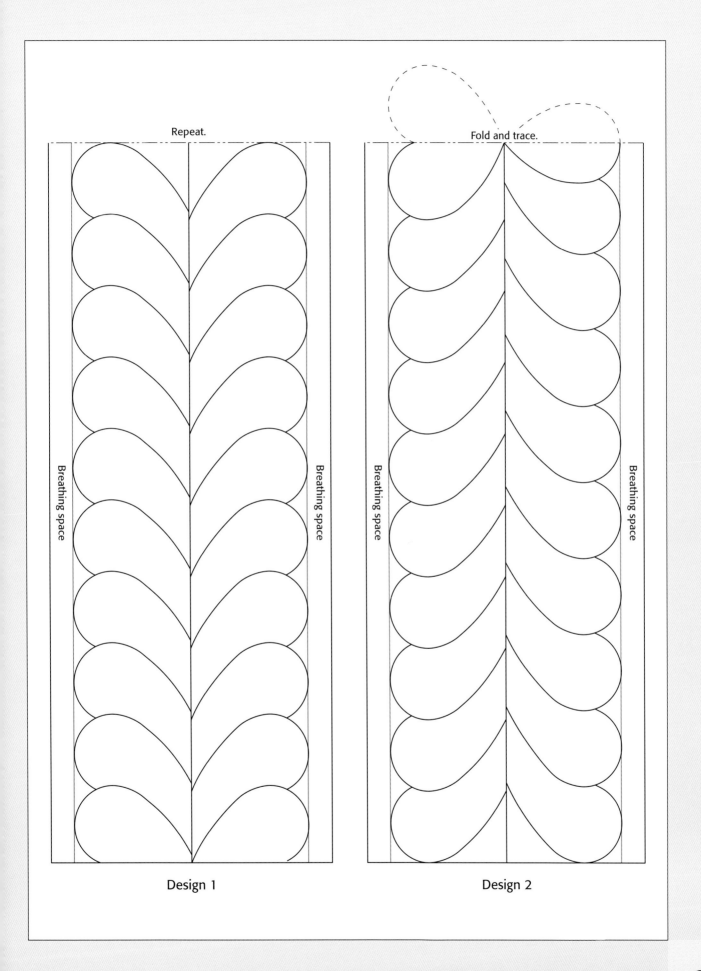

Repeat.

Fold and trace.

Breathing space

Breathing space

Breathing space

Breathing space

Design 1

Design 2

Marking the Quilt Top

Refer to the illustration below for steps 1–7.

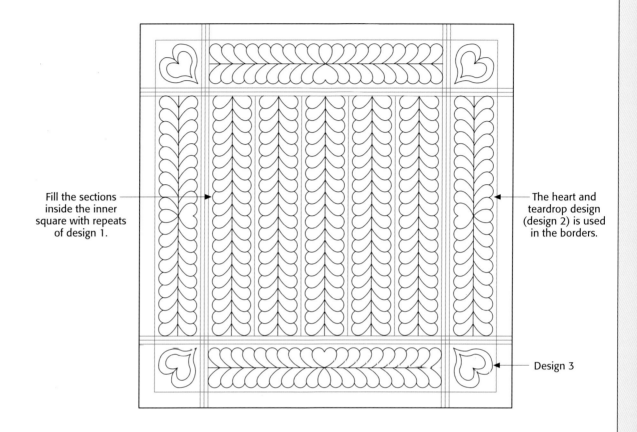

Fill the sections inside the inner square with repeats of design 1.

The heart and teardrop design (design 2) is used in the borders.

Design 3

1. Using a fabric-marking pen or pencil, draw a 15" square in the center of the 24" fabric square. Draw a 16" square with the lines ½" outside the lines of the 15" square. Finally, draw a 22" square with the lines 3" beyond the lines of the 16" square.

2. Divide the 15" square into five 3" x 15" rectangles and mark. These are the areas where you will draw the straight-spine feather design (design 1, page 21).

3. Using the paper pattern you made for the straight-spine feathers, transfer the design into each rectangle and repeat the pattern to fill out each one (see "Transferring Quilting Designs" on page 136).

4. Extend the lines of the 15" and 16" squares out to the 22" square. Then add a third line halfway between these 2 lines. The lines should be ¼" apart. They define the inside square and create the square spaces for the corner designs.

5. Trace the heart at right onto paper and then transfer the design onto each corner of the quilt top.

6. Transfer the border design into the 3"-wide areas around the outer edge of the fabric square (design 2, page 21). Don't forget to flip the pattern to trace the opposite half of the design from the center point.

7. Draw a line ¼" outside the 22" square. This gives you an accurate positioning line for the binding. It's easier to mark it while the fabric is still flat (unquilted).

Quilting and Finishing

1. Layer the quilt top with batting and backing, and then pin baste the layers together.

Breathing space

Design 3

2. Attach a walking foot to your machine or engage the even-feed feature if available.

3. Quilt all the straight lines first. This includes the lines that define the center section, the lines that divide the rows of straight-spine feathers, and the spines of the feathers. Do not quilt the "breathing space" lines. These should never be drawn on the quilt top because they are only guidelines for drawing the designs.

4. After completing all the straight-line quilting, drop or disengage the feed dogs and attach a darning foot. Free-motion quilt the feathers and the corner hearts (see "Free-Motion Machine Quilting" on page 137 and "Machine Quilting Feathers" on page 140).

5. From the binding fabric, cut 3 strips, each 2" x 40", for the binding and 1 strip, 8" x 22", for the hanging sleeve.

6. Bind the quilt and add a hanging sleeve and label (see page 143).

   Congratulations! You've just finished your first feathered quilt!

NOTE: Grids and straight lines of quilting are great companions for feathered quilting designs. When you choose a grid for a border, it helps define the areas of feathers. If you choose one as background filling, it makes the feathers more pronounced by flattening the background areas.

Using these two simple feather designs with grids or straight lines gives you the opportunity to play with the outcome to create a variety of different quilt tops.

Practice Project 2:
Straight-Spine Feathers Variation Wall Hanging

Finished Quilt Size: 22½" x 22½"

Materials

See "Materials" for practice project 1 on page 20.

Marking and Completing the Quilt

Refer to the illustration below for steps 1–4.

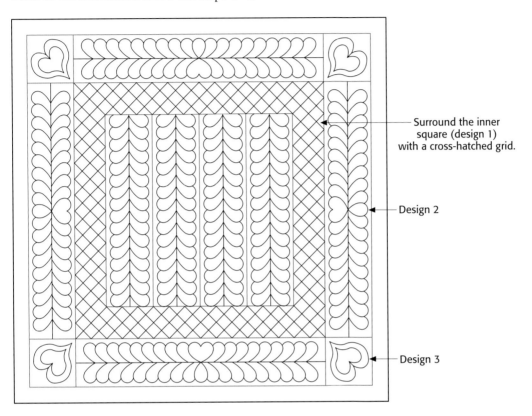

Surround the inner square (design 1) with a cross-hatched grid.

Design 2

Design 3

1. In the center of the 24" fabric square, draw a 12" square surrounded by a 16" and a 22" square.

2. Divide and mark the 12" square into four 3" x 12" rectangles for the straight-spine feather pattern (design 1, page 21).

3. Draw a 1" diagonal grid in the 2"-wide borders that surround the central square. Mark dots 1" apart on both sides of the lines defining the area. Then join the dots on the diagonal to form continuous lines that zigzag around the border. This grid will be easy to machine quilt with very few starts and stops.

4. Mark designs 2 (page 21) and 3 (page 23) in the outer border.

5. Refer to "Quilting and Finishing" on page 23 to complete the wall hanging.

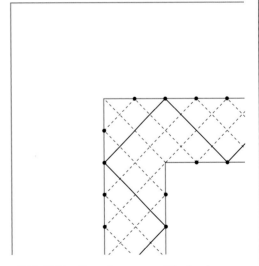

Grid stitching lines zigzag around the border.

CHAPTER 2

Feathered wreaths

If you've done the workbook exercises so far and tried your hand at drawing and quilting straight-spine feathers in a small wall hanging, you are ready to move on to the next technique—drawing feathers around a circle to create a feathered wreath.

Drawing Feathers around a Circle

Although you may think this looks more difficult, the basic technique for drawing feathered circles isn't much different from drawing straight-spine feathers—you just draw them along a curved spine instead of a straight one, with an inner circle and an outer circle as the height lines.

Exercise 1: Just Tracing

1. Place a clean sheet of paper on top of the feathered wreath on page 27. Use a drawing compass to trace the 3 circles for the spine and height lines.

2. Ignoring the ruler lines on the illustration for now, carefully trace the feathers in the design. Because the feathers are in a circle you can begin with any feather. Begin drawing each new feather from the outside curve of the feather that just precedes it.

Exercise 2: Drawing Feathers in a Circle

Drawing feathers on a circular line rather than a straight line presents its own challenges and will take some practice. Each feather still has a starting point and the point where it touches the spine, in line and perpendicular to it.

1. On a clean sheet of paper, trace the circular spine and height lines for the wreath, using a compass set at radii that match those in the illustration.

2. Use a small coin to draw the "tops" of the feathers along the height lines. When you are close to completing the circle, very lightly draw the last few coin tops to make sure they will all fit. You may discover that you cannot complete the final coin top. If you draw a feather for an incomplete coin top, the resulting feather will be very skinny. Since all of the feathers should be about the same size, you will need to make an adjustment. You will have to "fudge" to make full feathers fit around the circle so that all the feathers appear to be the same size. See "Fudging the Feathers" on page 28.

3. To make drawing the feather a little less daunting, place one edge of a small ruler at the beginning of the feather (beginning of the coin top) and at the compass center point as shown on the facing page. The point where the ruler crosses the spine line is the point where the feather will finish. It's just that simple! Use a colored pencil to make a small mark on the spine line at this point so

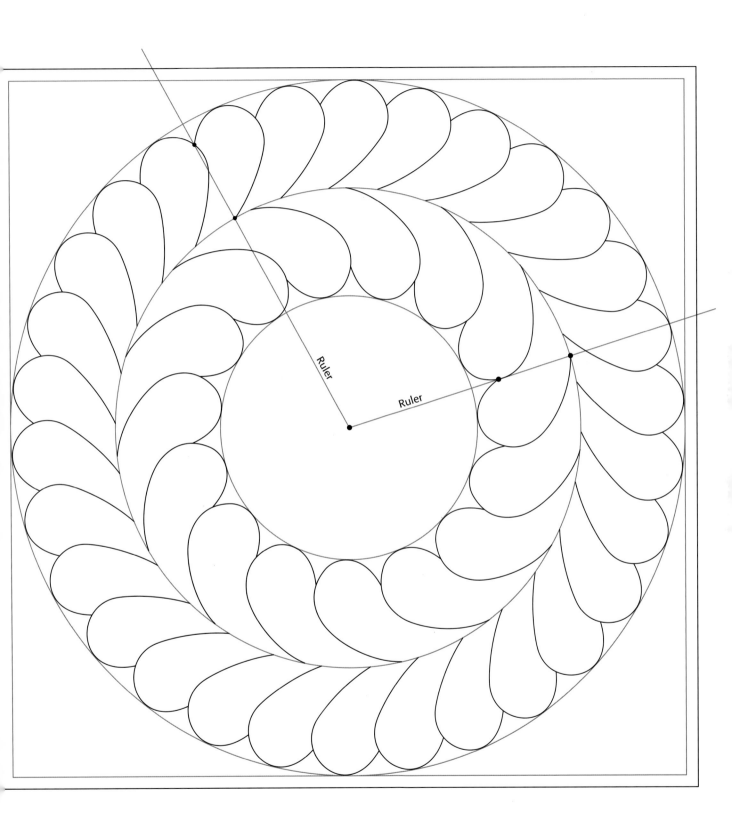

Ruler

Ruler

FUDGING THE FEATHERS

It will probably take a few trials to learn how to fudge feathers to fit around a circle. Here's how:

1. Erase the last 4 coin tops you drew, but before you do, look at the little triangular space between the coin tops and the height line—the shaded area in the illustration below.

2. Make the space between coin tops a little smaller by overlapping the coins a little. To make it larger, draw a little farther around each coin top.

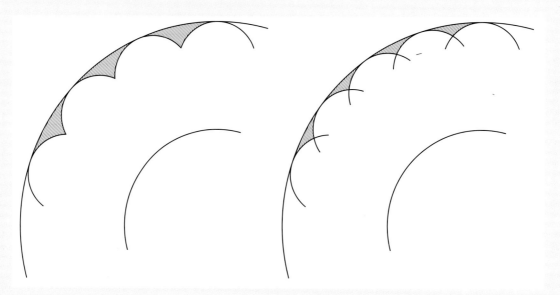

Note: Avoid the temptation to try to fudge only the last one or two feathers. Spreading the correction out over four or five feathers (coin tops) is far less noticeable.

FUNNY FEATHERS

If the feathers on the inside of the wreath look "funny" and you are sure you followed all the guidelines, adjust them by making the curve of the feathers where they come down to touch the spine appear to flow or follow the curve of the spine a bit more. It's OK to bend the rule for a more pleasing visual result.

that you can see where you are heading as you draw each feather. To avoid confusion, use a different color to mark the point for the feathers that you will draw on the other side of the spine.

4. Choose one of the coin tops you drew and begin drawing the first feather, from the coin top down around the curve and then to the spine.

5. Draw the second feather, beginning at the outside curve of the one you just completed. Draw around the coin top and down to the spine. Repeat the process until you have completed all feathers on one side of the spine.

6. Draw feathers on the other side of the spine in the same manner, making sure the feathers travel in the same direction around the spine. If your feathers form Ss across the spine, they are going in different directions. Note that the inside ring will have a different number of feathers than the outside ring (the inside circle is smaller).

Practice Project 3:
Feathered Wreath Pillow Covers

Feathered Wreath Cushion (Design 4), 15½" x 15½"

Feathered Wreath Cushion (Design 5), 15½" x 15½"

Feathered Wreath Cushion (Design 6), 15½" x 15½"

Feathered Wreath Cushion (Design 7), 15½" x 15½"

Traditional feathered wreaths make beautiful pillow (cushion) tops like these. They make the perfect small project on which to practice your drawing and quilting techniques. They also offer lots of opportunity for design experimentation.

Allow your imagination free rein as you experiment with drawing your own feathered wreath designs for pillow covers and small hangings. Altering the position of the spine—closer to the center or closer to the outer edges of the square—results in very different feathered wreaths, as shown in the photographs on page 29. Using different feather widths also creates different effects. A double feather wreath—one inside another—is especially beautiful. And there's nothing to say that you can't do a feather wreath with feathers on only one side of the spine or a wreath with fat feathers on one side of the spine and skinnier feathers on the other. Adding diagonal grids, stippling, or echo quilting inside and/or outside of the feather wreaths adds more interest and dimension to the completed work.

If you don't like some of your experimental drawings, examine them to determine what isn't working so that you can make adjustments in your next drawings. The point is to learn something new—and have fun doing it!

Materials for 1 Pillow Cover
17" square of fabric for the pillow top
19" square of fabric for the backing
18" square of fabric for pillow cover back
19" square of batting
14"-long nylon coil zipper
16" pillow form*

The form is ½" larger than the finished pillow cover to ensure a snug fit for a plump pillow that fills out the corners of the cover. If you prefer a softer, flatter pillow, make a 15" square, muslin pillow cover and stuff with polyester fiberfill to the desired fullness. Sew the muslin pillow form closed and tuck it inside the finished pillow cover.

Drawing the Wreaths
Draw your own feathered wreath design as directed below or use one of the designs provided (see pages 35–38). Enlarge it by 200 percent on a photocopier (see page 9).

1. Using a clean sheet of paper for each of the 4 designs, draw a 14½" square and then draw a 15" square outside the first, centering it carefully so that there is ¼" of "breathing space" all around the inner square. Your feathered designs must stay inside this 14½" square design area on each sheet.

2. Mark the center of each square by drawing diagonal lines from corner to corner. Mark the point where the lines intersect with a visible black dot.

3. Place the point of a drawing compass on the black dot to draw a circle that touches the inner square—a circle with a radius of 7¼".

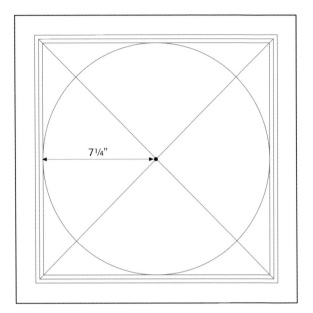

7¼"

4. Referring to the chart and the illustrations, draw additional circles inside the first one for each of the 4 designs.

Circle	Design 4 Radius	Design 5 Radius	Design 6 Radius	Design 7 Radius
2	5"	4¼"	5 ¼"	5½"
3	2¾"	2¾"	5"	4"
4			3½"	3¾"
5			2"	2¾"
6			1¾"	1¾"

5. Study the squares you've drawn for each of the 4 designs to identify the spine(s) and the height lines in each one (see pages 35–38).

6. Using an appropriately sized coin top, draw feathers on both sides of the spine line in each design, making note that the outer spine in design 6 has feathers only on the outer edge and not on the inner edge.

Adjust your design drawings until you are pleased with the results.

NOTE: An "appropriately sized coin top" is one that gives you a feather that doesn't look squashed between the height and spine lines. Some sizes will look better than others. For example, in design 7 on page 38 I used a small coin top for the inner feather wreath. Anything larger would not have fit to create a pleasing feather. Now compare the outer ring of feathers in designs 4 and 5. A larger coin

MARKING AN ACCURATE QUILTING GRID

To draw a diagonal grid behind your feather wreaths, mark dots at 1" intervals on each side of the 15" square. Then join the dots on the diagonal, working from the corners out. This method ensures a perfect grid rather than one with spaces between the lines that are not equal. This grid-marking error (a parallax error) often happens when you simply slide a rotary ruler across the area, marking as you go.

The method for drawing a grid is the same for a square or rectangular space as well as for a border. First you must determine the grid size that best fits the length and width of the area to be quilted in a grid pattern.

Since the measurements of a square are the same on all four sides, determining the grid size is easy. If the size of the grid (the distance between the grid lines, 1" for example) will divide evenly into the length of a side, you can use that grid size. If it doesn't divide evenly, you need to use a different size. For example, a 2" grid won't work on a 15" square because it doesn't divide evenly. However, a 1", 1½", or 3" grid works for a 15" square.

Rectangles are a bit more complicated because the width and length measurements are different. To determine an appropriate grid size, you must find a number that will divide evenly into *both* dimensions with no fractions. For example, a 2" grid won't work for a 10" x 15" rectangle because 2 doesn't divide evenly into 15. A 1" or a 2½" grid will work, however.

After you determine the appropriate grid size, mark dots along all edges, using the grid size as the measurement. Beginning at a corner, join the dots on the diagonal or in straight lines as you prefer to make a grid that fits perfectly in the area to be quilted.

Borders require three sets of measurements. You must measure the length of the inside and outside edge (seam line) of the border strip as well as the width of the border and then find a number that divides evenly into all three measurements. For example, if your 2½"-wide border measures 20" at the inside edge and 25" at the outside edge, you could not use a 2" grid because it does not divide evenly into 25" or 2½". However, a ½", 1¼", or 2½" grid would work with all three dimensions.

NOTE: If the quilt is rectangular, the grid size must divide evenly into the width and the inner and outer border measurements of both borders.

After determining the grid size for a border, mark dots that distance apart along the inside and outside sewing lines. Beginning in a corner, join the dots on the diagonal around the entire border in both directions to create the grid. This creates lines that you can quilt continuously, zigzag fashion, around all four sides of a quilt as discussed in "Straight-Spine Feathers Variation Wall Hanging" on page 25.

top was used for both, but because the distance from the spine to the height line is larger in design 5, the coin tops actually appear smaller.

7. Go over the final designs with a dark permanent pen. Be sure to mark the spine line(s), the lines for the breathing space, and the lines for the outer square.

Marking the Pillow Cover Top

1. Using the feathered design of your choice, transfer the design to the center of a 17" fabric square (see "Transferring Quilting Designs" on page 136).

2. If you want to add grids in the areas surrounding the wreath, mark them now, referring to the directions in the box on the facing page.

3. I draw a binding positioning line ¼" beyond the 15" square because I like to bind my pillows in the same way I bind a quilt. The project will finish to 15½" square when bound, and the pillow cover will have a knife-edge finish.

Quilting the Pillow Cover Top

1. Layer the marked pillow top with the 19" squares of batting and backing fabric; pin baste the layers together.

2. Attach the darning foot, drop or cover the feed dogs, and free-motion machine quilt the spine line(s) (see "Free-Motion Machine Quilting" on page 137 and "Machine Quilting Feathers" on page 140). Next, quilt the feathers.

3. If desired, use the darning foot to do free-motion stippling, as shown for the pillow made using design 7 (see page 29).

4. If you are stitching a grid pattern in the open spaces of the pillow cover, raise the feed dogs and attach a walking foot to your machine or engage the even-feed feature.

Finishing the Pillow Cover

NOTE: I finish my pillow covers just like a quilt, with a binding that creates a knife-edge finish.

1. From the 18" square for the pillow back, cut a 4" x 18" strip.

2. With right sides together and using a ¾"-wide seam allowance, stitch the 4" x 18" strip to the 14" x 18" piece. To begin, stitch the first 2" of the seam and backstitch a few stitches. Without breaking the threads, change to a basting-length stitch (6 stitches per inch). Continue stitching the next 14". Change to a normal stitch length, take a few stitches, backstitch, and continue to the edge to complete the seam. Press the seam open.

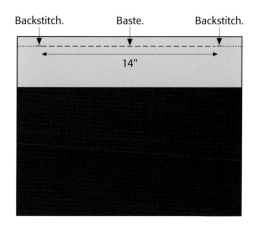

Backstitch.   Baste.   Backstitch.

14"

3. Insert a zipper in the 14"-long basted section, using a lapped zipper technique so that the coil is not exposed in the finished pillow back.

4. Place the quilted cushion top face up on the wrong side of the pillow cover back.

5. Position the raw edges of the binding along the outer marked line and sew the binding in place with a ¼"-wide seam as you would on a small quilt.

Lapped zipper

6. Trim both the pillow top and backing even with the binding raw edges. Hand sew the binding to the back of the pillow.

7. Unzip the pillow cover and insert the pillow form. Zip the zipper.

Design 4
Enlarge 200%.

Design 5
Enlarge 200%.

Design 6
Enlarge 200%.

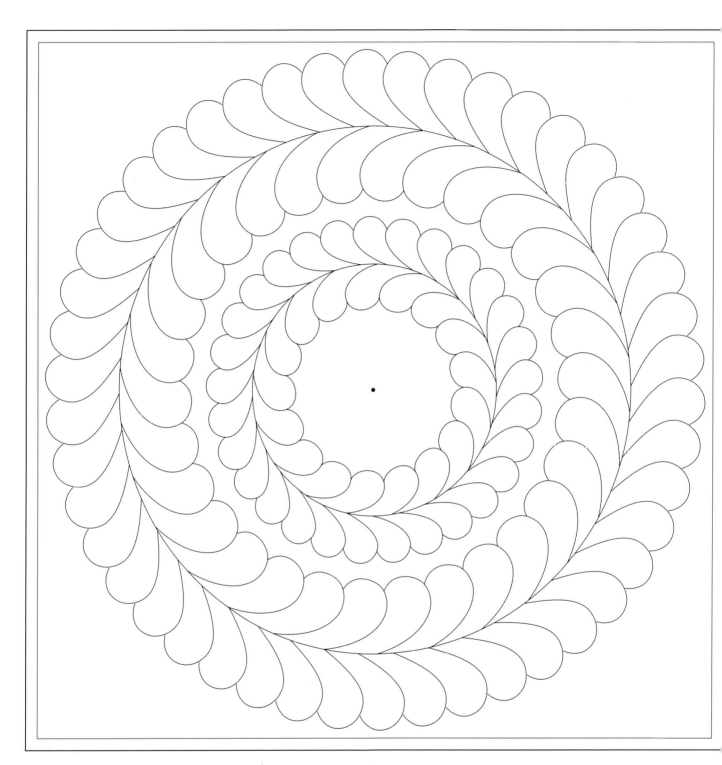

Design 7
Enlarge 200%.

Practice Project 4:
Small Amish Wall Hanging

Finished Size: 30" x 30"

This small quilt features a simple pieced design embellished with straight-spine
feather designs and a central feathered wreath.

Combine straight-spine feathers and a feathered wreath, add some crosshatching, and all of a sudden you are designing feathered quilts. Amish colors and designs are splendid for showing off feathered quilting patterns. This small wall hanging is no exception.

Materials

Yardage is based on 42"-wide fabric, with 40" of usable width after preshrinking.

¾ yd. purple fabric for the quilt center and binding
⅓ yd. navy fabric for the corner triangles
½ yd. green fabric for the borders
1⅛ yds. fabric for the backing and hanging sleeve
34" x 34" square of batting

Cutting

From the purple fabric, cut:
  1 piece, 15½" square
  4 pieces, 4½" square
  4 strips, 2" x 40"
From the navy fabric, cut:
  2 pieces, 11½" square; cut once diagonally for a total of 4 triangles.
From the green fabric, cut:
  4 strips, 4½" x 21¾"
From the backing fabric, cut:
  1 piece, 34" square
  1 strip, 6" x 30"

Piecing the Quilt Top

All seam allowances are ¼" wide.

1. Sew a navy triangle to opposite edges of the large purple square. Press the seams toward the triangles. Repeat with the remaining navy triangles.

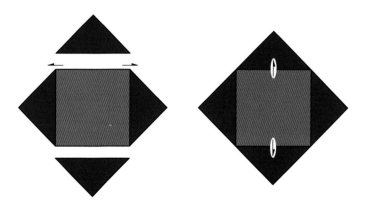

2. Sew a green strip to opposite edges of the center square with triangles. Press the seams toward the borders.

3. Sew a purple square to each end of the 2 remaining green border strips. Press the seams toward the green strips.

Make 2.

4. Sew the pieced border strips to the remaining edges of the center square and press toward the borders.

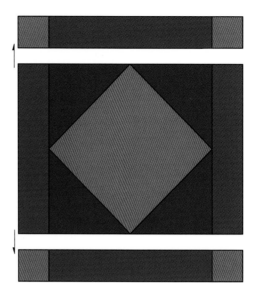

Drawing the Feathers

Use design 8 for the borders and design 9 for the corners (see page 43 and below), or draw your own feather patterns. Choose any one of the feathered wreath designs (4, 5, 6, or 7) for the center square.

1. To draw the border design, refer to design 2 on page 21, but draw a 4¼" x 10⅝" rectangle. Draw a breathing space line ¼" inside one of the long edges of the rectangle. Draw a line ½" inside the other long edge of the rectangle to allow for ¼" for binding and ¼" for breathing space. The resulting design area should measure 3½" x 10⅝". Since this is only half of the border length, you will need to flip and

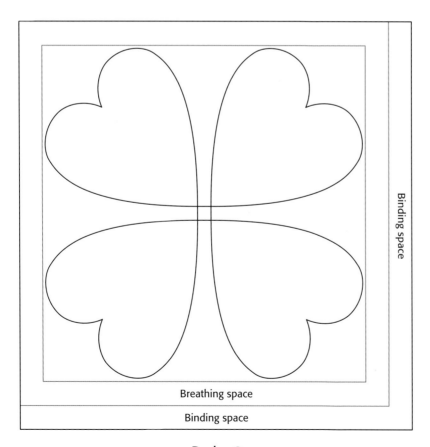

Binding space

Breathing space

Binding space

Design 9

trace the design in the second half of the border. Follow the directions on page 13 for "Drawing Hearts and Teardrops" to draw this larger feather design. Use a medium-sized coin for the feather tops. Go over the finished design with a dark permanent marker.

2. Use design 9 (page 41) for the corner.

Marking the Quilt Top

1. Transfer the completed designs to the appropriate areas of the completed quilt top (see page 136).

2. Draw 1" crosshatching in the navy triangles. Orient the crosshatching on the diagonal or draw it vertically and horizontally as in the illustration below.

Quilting and Finishing

1. Layer the quilt top with batting and backing; pin baste the layers together.

2. Attach the walking foot or engage the even-feed feature if available. Stitch in the ditch of all the seam lines first to define the quilting areas. This stitching also helps to stabilize the areas to be quilted. Complete any other straight lines of stitching and then quilt the feather spines.

3. Drop or cover the feed dogs and attach the darning foot. Choose thread to match the fabric color. Machine quilt the feathers and the corner designs (see "Free-Motion Machine Quilting" on page 137 and "Machine Quilting Feathers" on page 140). Remove the basting pins.

4. Bind the quilt and add a hanging sleeve and label (see pages 142–143).

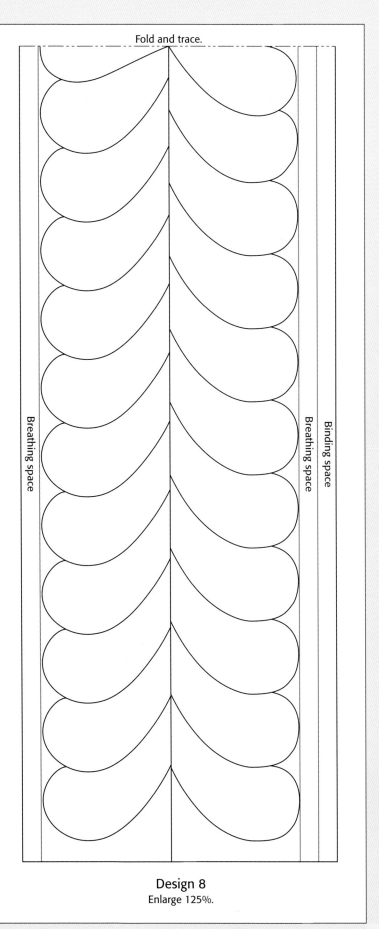

Fold and trace.

Breathing space

Breathing space

Binding space

Design 8
Enlarge 125%.

CHAPTER 3

Curved border repeats

Using a design-area repeat allows you to work out a section of the design and then use it over and over again to fill a specific space with a continuous design. Just a little math is required in order to design and draw feathers for border repeats. Don't let the *M* word scare you, though. A simple calculator is all you need to master this technique. Take the time to work through the exercise below and you will have finished designs for a beautiful small quilt that is all your own.

In this chapter and the one that follows, I have provided set measurements for the repeats and corners to make it easier for you to learn to draw them. After you've practiced a bit and understand how to use a repeat and the options for turning corners, we'll do the math so that you will be able to apply what you've learned to determine the correct repeat for any quilt.

Drawing Repeats

We will use "Amish Bars Quilt 1" on page 55—the practice project for this chapter—as an example to work through the process of drawing a repeat. For this quilt, one of the repeat sizes is 5½" x 10".

1. Draw a 5½" x 10" rectangle on a clean sheet of paper.

2. Draw lines for breathing space ¼" from each long edge inside the rectangle. Breathing space is not required at the short ends where the repeat will join the next one to continue unbroken. The resulting design area should be 5" x 10".

3. Draw a line through the center of the design space, halfway between the two breathing-space lines. Draw lines across the center line to divide the space into 8 sections of equal length. Each section in this design should measure 2½" x 2½" (not all repeats will make these sections square.)

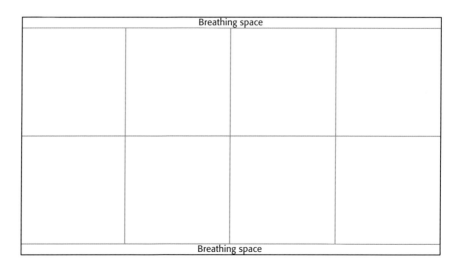

4. To draw the curve for a repeat, start with the lower left-hand section of the design area and make a mark halfway up on the left-hand side. From this mark, draw a smooth curve to the upper right-hand corner of the same section. The curve should flow smoothly from your mark, without dropping below it or rising sharply at an angle. It should curve up to cut the corner at a 45° angle.

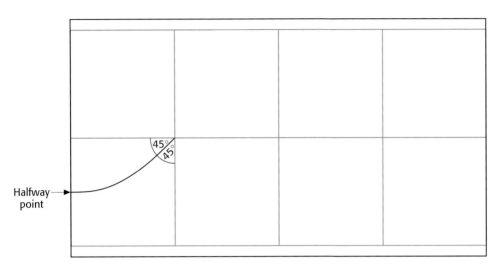

Halfway point

5. Position a clean sheet of tracing paper that is about twice the size of this section on top of the curve you've just drawn. Trace the outline of the section and the curve with a dark marker.

6. Rotate the tracing paper 180° and place it under the original drawing. Line it up with the second upper left section of the design space and trace the curve into this section.

7. Fold the rectangle in half crosswise and trace the curves onto the other half of the rectangle. When you unfold the paper once again, you will have a curve that flows smoothly across the design area as shown below. You have just drawn the spine line for a feathered border repeat.

NOTE: This repeat, composed of two half bottom curves and one full top curve, remains constant for any design you use that requires a repeat. When you join two repeats, the half bottom curves join and make a full curve so the design can flow smoothly into the next repeat. (That is why there are no breathing spaces at the short ends of a repeat.)

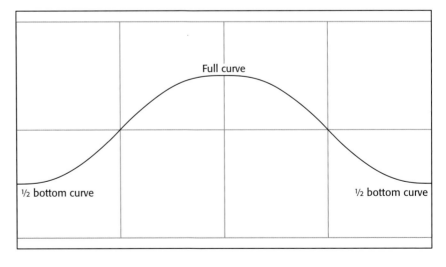

Full curve

½ bottom curve   ½ bottom curve

8. To add height lines so that you can draw feathers along the curved spine, measure from the beginning of the spine to the line for the breathing space along the edge of the lower left section. In this example, that distance is 1¼" and is the same on both sides of the spine along the entire repeat.

Use a ruler to make a series of marks about ¼" apart on each side of the spine. Position the ruler so that it is perpendicular to the spine for each mark. Extend the height lines past the lower left section outline to an imaginary line that crosses the center dividing line at a 45° angle (The imaginary line is perpendicular to the curving spine line.) This is necessary so that you can align the height lines when you trace them into the next section.

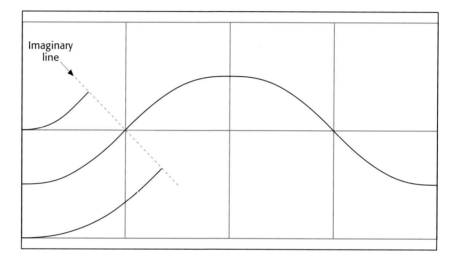

9. Now do the same tracing as in steps 5 and 6, but this time include the height lines. Then fold and trace as in step 7 to get all the lines needed onto the design area. Your design area should look like the illustration on facing page. Now that you understand

the procedure, if you begin by drawing both the spine and the height lines in the first section, you will need to do only 1 tracing to get all of the required lines for the repeat curve.

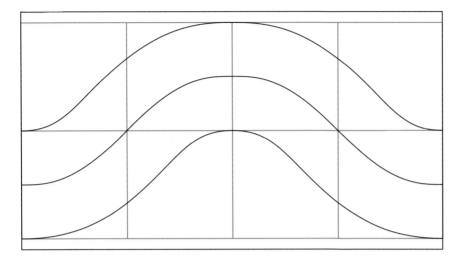

10. Draw feathers along the spine on both sides. It is essential that you draw a complete feather at the beginning of the repeat and a complete feather curve just touching the other end of the repeat. If you don't, the feathers won't be complete where you connect the repeats. It's like making the feathers fit the circle of the feather wreath; if you have only a half feather at either end, the design doesn't flow or repeat itself.

Using a small coin, mark coin tops along both height lines. Make sure you have full coin tops at both ends of the repeat, fudging to fit as necessary (see "Fudging the Feathers" on page 28). Draw the feathers, keeping in mind that the imaginary line through the beginning of the feather and the point where the feather touches the spine is at right angles to the spine line. The feathers will change angle slightly as the curve of the spine changes, in much the same way

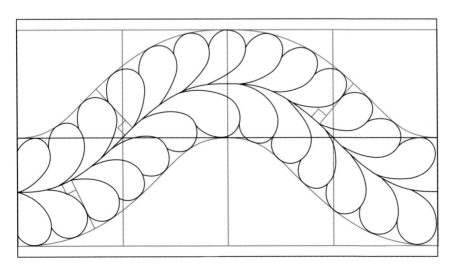

they do when drawing a feathered wreath (page 26). Unfortunately, there is no compass point to guide you, so you will need to rely on your eye. Make sure that the feathers begin at the same end of the repeat—no S curves, please.

Intertwining Double Feather Repeat

1. Follow the "Drawing Repeats" procedure outlined beginning on page 44 to draw the spine and height lines for the length of the repeat.

2. Fold the rectangle in half lengthwise and trace onto both sides any lines that are not already drawn in each half. The result is a mass of lines. Making sense of these lines reveals the intertwining, over-under pattern to follow when drawing the feathers. You will erase the lines you don't need.

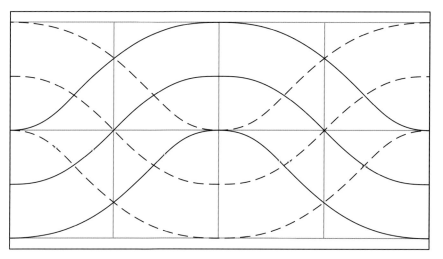

Trace all lines on both halves of the repeat pattern.

3. Using the illustration on the following page, place 2 fingers (1 within each height line) on each side of the spine in the bottom left-hand section at the outer end of the rectangle. Moving your fingers from left to right, follow the

curve for half of the repeat to the center line. Erase any lines that your fingers touch as they pass over the design.

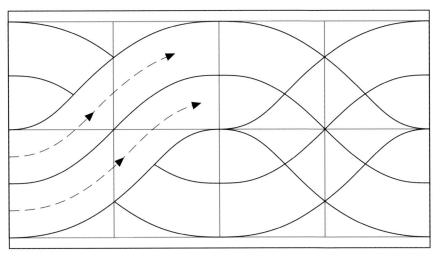

Move your fingers from the left to the center line.
Erase lines your fingers cross.

4. Lift your fingers from the above illustration and place them within the height lines on each side of the spine in the lower section that is third from the left, beginning at the center line. Moving from left to right, follow the curve with your fingers to the end of the repeat and erase any lines that your fingers pass over. Now you have 2 separate curves that intertwine at each of the vertical lines.

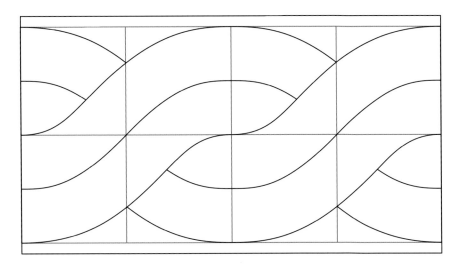

5. For more distinct intertwining, most designs have a small gap in the center of the 2 curves. (Look at the illustration at the top of page 51.) Decide how large you want the gap—in this case 1" is suitable. (The wider the design, the larger the gap can be.) Draw another 5½" x 10" rectangle on a clean sheet of paper,

draw the lines for the breathing space, and draw the spine and height lines, allowing for the gap as described in steps 6–8 below.

6. For a 1" center gap, mark half that distance down from the upper left corner of the lower left-hand section. Then mark the halfway point from there to the breathing-space line at the bottom edge (1" in this example). Begin the spine at this point and curve to the upper right-hand corner of the section as you did for the previous drawing. Add height lines on each side of the spine—1" from the spine in this example.

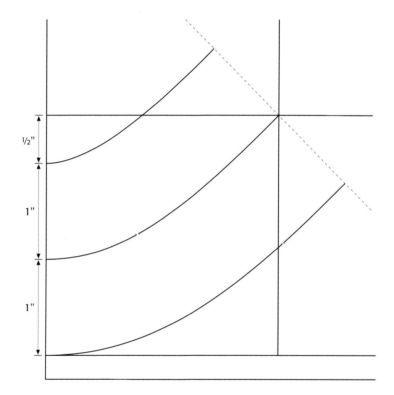

7. Continue as directed above, tracing all the curves and then folding the rectangle in half lengthwise. Trace again. Like magic, you will have a 1" gap at the center of the curves.

8. Erase the lines you don't need as directed above, and then use a small coin to draw the top curves of the feathers along the height lines. Where the feathers appear to go underneath the other curve, draw them as they fall without

concern about whether they are full or partial feathers. However, you must have a full feather at the beginning and end of the repeat so that you will have full feathers along the entire border when you trace the repeats on your quilt top.

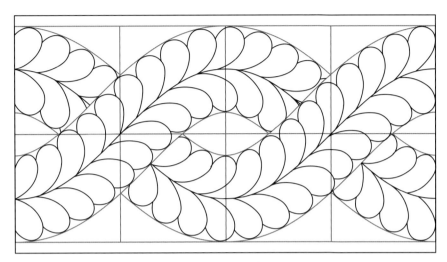

Intertwining Double Feather Repeat

NOTE: The gap between the intertwining feathers can be any width you wish. Choose the distance you want, halve the amount, and then measure and make a mark at this point, down from the lengthwise center line at the edge of the design area. Divide the remaining distance from this mark to the breathing-space line in half. Begin the spine at that point.

Drawing Cables

You may realize by now that in addition to learning how to draw intertwining feather designs, you have also learned how to draw cables. The spine and the height lines are cables!

The wider the border, the greater the distance between the spine line and the height lines. If you are drawing feathers, the wider the border the larger the feathers will be.

If you are drawing cables, you may want more lines between the spine line and the height lines. Divide the area between the lines in halves or quarters and draw lines that are equidistant from each other along the entire length.

It is easier to leave out the unders and overs for machine quilted cables, so that the continuous lines form small grids where they cross. This eliminates starts and stops in your quilting, making the work go faster.

1.   Draw a 5½" x 10" rectangle on a piece of tracing paper divided up for a repeat. Using a 1" gap between the curves as directed on pages 49–50, draw a spine line with height lines on each side of it.

2. Add another line on each side of the spine and equidistant from both the spine and height lines.

3. Fold the paper lengthwise and trace again.

4. Leave all the lines you have traced. This creates a cable with 5 lines that form a grid where all lines cross each other (see design 10 on page 53). Set aside to use for the next practice project.

Combining Cables and Feathers

Combining cables and feathers, as shown in design 11 on page 54, creates one more design option using what you've already learned. If you choose to use design 11 rather than draw your own, enlarge it 125 percent on a photocopier to make it fit the design space inside a 6½" x 12" rectangle.

1. Beginning with a 6½" x 12" rectangle with a 6" x 12" design area, draw the same repeat with a 1" gap between the curves as directed for "Intertwining Double Feather Repeat" on pages 49–50.

2. Trace all the lines and erase the necessary lines to create the overs and unders. Make 1 curve a cable with 5 lines and on the other draw feathers, making sure that the repeat begins and ends with a full feather. Set this design aside for the next project. Are you still with me? If you follow the illustrations with the step-by-step directions as you draw, it really isn't difficult at all.

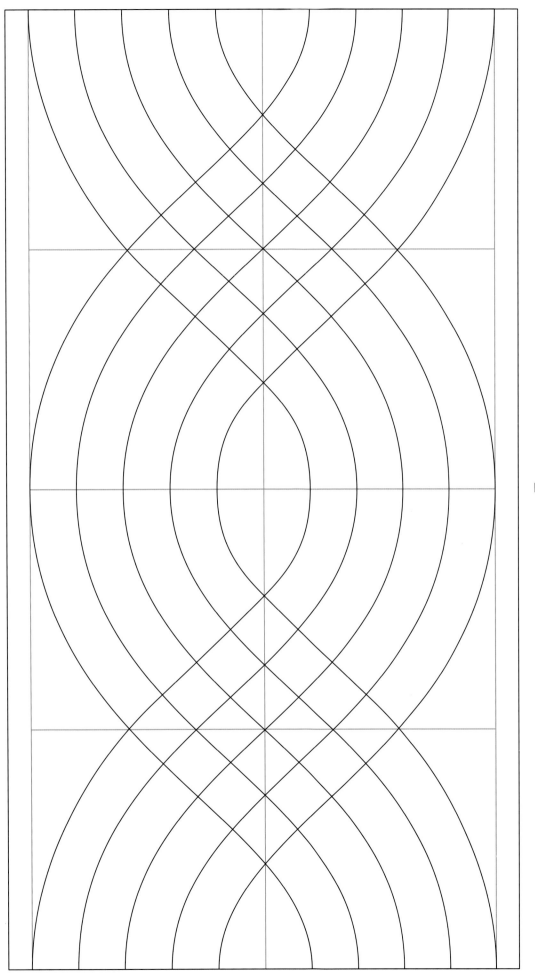

Design 10

Design 11
Enlarge 125%.

Practice Project 5:
Amish Bars Quilt 1

Finished Size: 37½" x 37½"
In this traditional Amish quilt, the border design runs to the edges with no attempt to turn the corners with the feathered design. This quilting style is often found in older quilts.

Amish quilts are simply pieced with plain-colored fabric, which makes them an excellent backdrop for lavish feathered quilting designs. If brights don't suit your taste, choose fabrics in more subtle or somber tones.

Materials

Yardage is based on 42"-wide fabric, with 40" of usable width after preshrinking

⅞ yd. red for the wide center strips and the outer border
⅝ yd. bright aqua for the inner border and binding
½ yd. bright pink for the narrow center strips and border corners
1½ yds. for the backing and hanging sleeve
42" x 42" square of batting

Cutting

From the red fabric, cut:
    2 strips, 6" x 20½", cutting along the fabric length
    4 strips, 7" x 24½"
From the bright pink fabric, cut:
    1 square 14" x 14"; cut into 4 squares, each 7" x 7"
    3 strips, 3½" x 20½"
From the bright aqua fabric, cut:
    2 strips, 2½" x 20½"
    2 strips, 2½" x 24½"
    4 strips, 2" x 40"
From the backing fabric, cut:
    1 piece, 40" square
    1 strip, 8" x 37"

Piecing the Quilt Top

All seam allowances are ¼" wide.

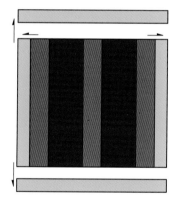

1. Sew the center strips together in an alternating fashion to create the center square. Press the seams toward the bright pink strips.

2. Sew the 20½"-long bright aqua strips to opposite sides of the center square and press the seams toward the bright aqua strips. Sew the 24½" bright aqua strips to the top and bottom edges of the center square and press toward the bright aqua strips.

3. Sew a long red strip to opposite sides of the quilt top and press the seams toward the strips.

4. Sew a bright pink square to opposite ends of two of the remaining red strips and press the seams toward the red strips. Sew to the top and bottom edges of the quilt top and press the seams toward the red strips.

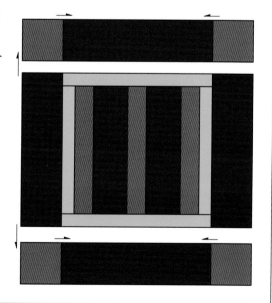

Drawing and Transferring the Feather Patterns

1. For the 3"-wide pink strips in the quilt-top center, trace or draw the straight-spine feather design 1 (page 21) onto tracing paper. Transfer to the quilt top, repeating to the length required in each strip.

2. For the 5½"-wide red center strips, use the cable repeat design 10 (page 53). Transfer to the strips, repeating the design twice in each strip.

3. Mark a 1" diagonal grid on the inner border (see page 32).

4. Use the feathered cable repeat design 11 (page 54) for the outer border. Three repeats will fit in the opposite side borders. Locate the center of each border and center the repeat there. Add a repeat on each side of the first repeat to complete the border pattern up to the breathing-space lines. Extend the quilting lines to the outer raw edges of the quilt so that you will not have starts and stops inside the quilt itself. Trace 2 repeats that fit exactly into each of the remaining borders (top and bottom). Your marked quilt top should look like the line drawing below.

NOTE: The border strips were cut 7" wide, allowing for ¼" seams to join the borders to the quilt top, plus ¼" of breathing space on each side of the quilting design, plus ¼" for binding the outer edges. That leaves a 6"-wide design area within the border strip.

Quilting and Finishing

1. Layer the quilt top with batting and backing, and then pin baste the layers together.

2. Attach the walking foot or engage the even-feed function if available. Stitch in the ditch of all the seam lines, except those where the cable flows across them into the corners. Next quilt all straight lines, including the grid in the inner border, the feather spines, and the cables (yes, I call cables straight lines).

3. Lower the feed dogs or disengage them and attach the darning foot. Machine quilt the feathers (see "Free-Motion Machine Quilting" on page 137 and "Machine Quilting Feathers" on page 140).

4. Bind the quilt and add a hanging sleeve and label (see page 143).

CHAPTER 4

Corners for continuous border designs

Now, at last, you will learn how to create feathered quilting patterns that flow continuously from one border, around the corner, and into the next border in an unbroken design.

Keep in mind that all repeats have two half bottom curves and one full top curve. This is a constant with repeats. Therefore, if you position the repeats the same way along the border, i.e., with the full curve at either the inner or the outer edge all along the quilt border, the design flows smoothly, in a continuous design. When the quilt is rectangular, the top and bottom borders will have a different number of repeats than the number required for the side borders. The repeat is always the same type of curve that you have learned to draw so far if you have worked through the drawing exercises in this book.

In the illustration below there are two different corner designs, showing what happens when you position the repeat with the full curve at the inside edge of the border or at the outside edge. Your quilt will have one or the other, never both, because these repeats are opposites.

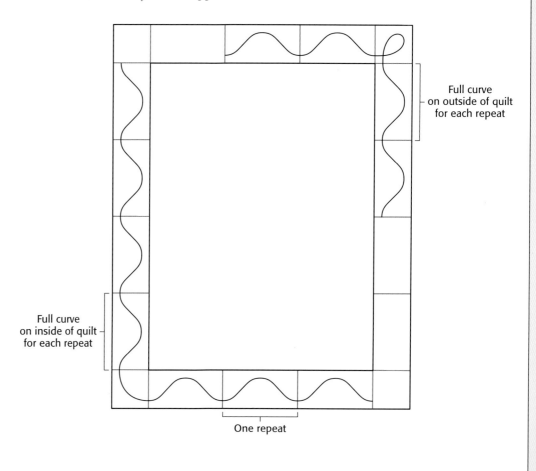

Full curve
on outside of quilt
for each repeat

Full curve
on inside of quilt
for each repeat

One repeat

To make a repeat design flow around a corner and continue into the next repeat, you must draw the corner as a separate design. If your borders are all the same width, as in most quilts, the corner will be a square.

Drawing the Corner Design

The example that follows is based on the Amish quilt project featured in the previous chapter. There are many ways to turn a corner and keep the design flowing, but for this corner, use the feathered cable from the Amish quilt as the repeat (design 11 on page 54) to draw a corner that continues the feathered cable.

1. Draw a 6½" square with a ¼" breathing space marked off inside 2 adjacent edges, which will be the outer corner.

2. Mark a ¼" breathing space around the inside corner as shown in the circled area of the illustration below. If you forget to mark this, your design will not turn the corner properly. Breathing space is not required on the remaining edges of the square because the design must flow over these edges into the border repeat for a continuous design.

3. Draw a diagonal line from the inner corner to the outer corner of the square.

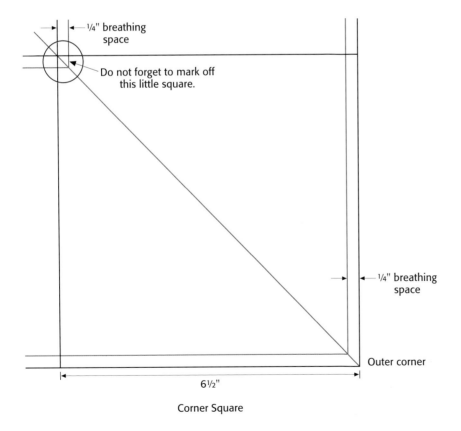

Corner Square

The feathers look best on the outside of the border corner, so the repeat must be placed with the full repeat curve of the feathers against the inner edge of the quilt.

4. On both edges that have no breathing space, mark dots that match the spine and height lines of the feathers and the 5 lines of the cable in the border repeat (design 11) where they meet the corner.

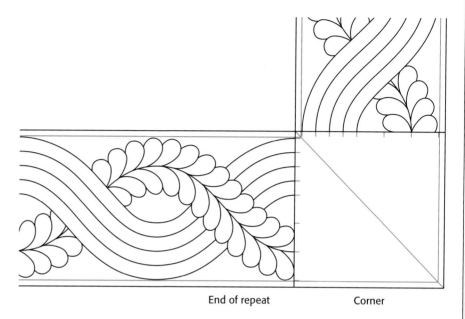

End of repeat   Corner

5. For the spine of the feathers, draw a smooth but slightly flat curved line around the corner, connecting the dots from one side of the corner to the other. *Do not use a compass to draw this curve.* Add height lines on either side of the spine that are the same distance from the spine as in the border repeat pattern.

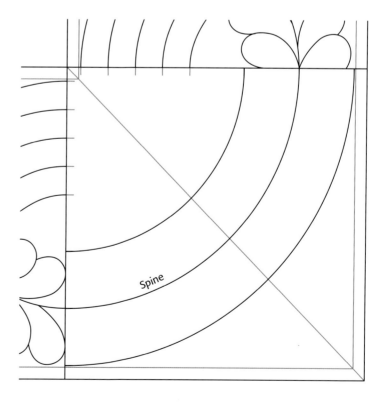

Spine

6. Draw coin tops around the corner, making them the same size as the ones in the repeat. Be sure to begin and end with full feathers at *both edges* of the corner square where it will join the border. Do *not* draw feathers beyond the corner design area; if you do, the corners will not flow into the border repeats.

7. Draw the cable in the corner as if it were a loop of ribbon going up under the feathers, folding back on itself under the feathers, and exiting again at the other inner edge of the corner. Draw the center line of the cable first so that it curves up to touch the feathers where the diagonal line cuts the corner in half. Draw the other cable lines equidistant from the center cable line. Fold the corner square in half along the diagonal line and trace these lines wherever you can see them on the square at both sides of the fold. This creates a grid (crosshatching) where the cable turns the corner, so the lines can be quilted continuously.

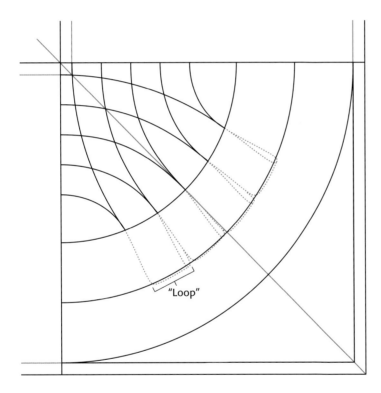

"Loop"

In the design used on the quilt, the cable appears opaque, so you do not see the grid. You see only the part of the cable that comes out from under itself to continue into the border repeat.

Design 12

Practice Project 6:
Amish Bars Quilt 2

Finished Size: 37½" x 37½"

Introducing a floral fabric to the traditional Amish quilt design and cutting the borders from a single fabric rather than using contrasting border corners results in a very different look. In this example, the feathered cable flows in a continuous pattern around the outer border. "Large Amish Bars Quilt" on page 133 of the gallery is a larger variation of this quilt design.

Except for the outer borders, the design and piecing for this quilt top are identical to "Amish Bars Quilt 1" on page 55. There are no corner squares in the outer border, and the feathered cable design flows continuously around the entire border. The patterned fabric in the inner border hides the grid quilting.

Materials

Yardage is based on 42"-wide fabric, with 40" of usable width after preshrinking.

1¼ yds. lavender fabric for the narrow center strips and the outer border
⅝ yd. coordinating print for the inner border and binding
⅜ yds. light lavender fabric for the wide center strips
1½ yds. fabric for the backing and hanging sleeve
42" x 42" square of batting

Cutting

From the lavender fabric, cut:
    3 strips, 3½" x 20½"
    2 strips, 7" x 24½"
    2 strips, 7"x 37½"
From the light lavender fabric, cut:
    2 strips, 6" x 20½"
From the print, cut:
    2 strips, 2½" x 20½"
    2 strips, 2½" x 24½"
    4 strips, 2" x 40"
From the backing fabric, cut:
    1 piece, 40" square
    1 strip, 8" x 37"

Piecing the Quilt Top

All seam allowances are ¼" wide.

1. Sew together the lavender and light lavender 20½"-long strips in an alternating fashion to create the center square. Press the seams toward the lavender strips.

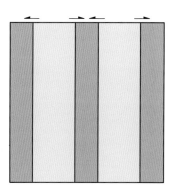

2. Sew the 20½"-long print strips to opposite sides of the center square and press the seams toward the print strips. Sew the 24½"-long print strips to the top and bottom edges of the center square and press toward the print strips.

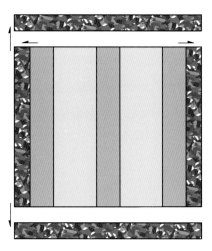

3. Sew the 24½"-long lavender strips to opposite sides of the quilt top. Press the seams toward the lavender strips. Sew the remaining lavender strips to the top and bottom edges of the quilt top. Press toward the lavender strips.

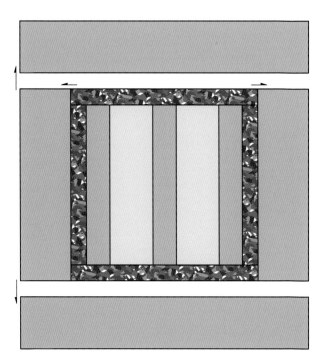

Drawing and Transferring the Feather Patterns

1. For the 3"-wide lavender strips in the quilt-top center, trace or draw the straight-spine feather design 1 (page 21) onto tracing paper. Transfer to the quilt top, repeating to the length required.

2. For the 5½"-wide light lavender center strips, use the cable repeat design 10 (page 53). Transfer to the strips, repeating the design twice in each strip.

3. Mark a 1" diagonal grid on the inner border (see page 32).

4. Use the feathered cable repeat design 11 (page 54) for the outer border. Position a repeat at each side of the center point in each border. Make sure that you have the full feathered curve of the repeat on the inner edge of the quilt so that the repeat will connect with the feathers at the outer edge of the corner.

5. Use the corner feathered cable pattern design 12 (page 62) in each corner to complete the border so that the design flows continuously around the border.

    Your marked quilt top should look like the drawing below.

Quilting and Finishing

1. Layer the quilt top with the batting and backing; pin baste the layers together.

2. Attach the walking foot or engage the even-feed function if available. Stitch in the ditch of all the seam lines except those where the cable flows across them into the border corners. Next quilt all straight lines, including the grid in the inner border, the feather spines, and all cable lines.

3. Lower or disengage the feed dogs and attach the darning foot. Machine quilt the feathers (see "Free-Motion Machine Quilting" on page 137 and "Machine Quilting Feathers" on page 140).

4. Bind the quilt and add a hanging sleeve and label (see page 143).

Practice Project 7:
White-on-White Whole-Cloth Quilt

Finished Size: 37½" x 37½"

Combining feather designs creates a stunning whole-cloth quilt. This wall hanging features the very same quilting designs used in "Amish Bars Quilt 2." Comparing the three Amish quilts is a great way to see how different a quilt can look when you simply change the fabrics.

Materials

Yardage is based on 42"-wide fabric, with 40" of usable width after preshrinking.

2¾ yds. white fabric for the quilt top, backing, hanging sleeve, and binding
42" x 42" square of batting

Cutting

From the white fabric, cut:
    1 square, 40" x 40"
    1 square, 42" x 42"
    4 strips, 2" x 40"
    1 strip, 8" x 37"

Marking the Quilt Top

1. Draw a 37" square, centering it on the 40" square of white fabric. Draw a 24" and a 20" square inside the first one.

2. Divide the 20" square into three 3" x 20" rectangles that alternate with two 5½" x 20" rectangles. (These lines are identical to the piecing lines in "Amish Bars Quilt 1" [page 55] and "Amish Bars Quilt 2" [page 63].)

3. Transfer the designs (design 1, page 21; design 10, page 53; design 11, page 54; and design 12, page 62) to the appropriate areas of the quilt top. Refer to the illustration on page 66 for placement.

4. Mark a grid in the 2"-wide border. Your marked quilt top should look like the line drawing on page 66.

Quilting and Finishing

1. Layer the quilt top with the batting and backing, and then pin baste the layers together.

2. Attach the walking foot or engage the even-feed function if available. Stitch in the ditch of all the seam lines except those where the cable flows across them into the border corners. Next quilt all straight lines, including the grid in the inner border, the feather spines, and all cable lines.

3. Lower the feed dogs or disengage them and attach the darning foot. Machine quilt the feathers (see "Free-Motion Machine Quilting" on page 137 and "Machine Quilting Feathers" on page 140).

4. Bind the quilt and add a hanging sleeve and label (see page 143).

CHAPTER 5

The math of repeats

Now that you've had some experience drawing repeats, it's time to learn how to apply what you've learned to designing a repeat for any border width and length. This is the exciting part! In this chapter, which could be subtitled "Or How to Figure Repeats for Any Border," you'll learn how easy it is to do the math required so you can draw designs for borders and sashing for *any quilt size* you make. It's also very freeing because you will never need another ready-made stencil or book pattern that isn't the right size and so requires tedious adjusting before you can use it.

Because the repeat curve is a constant, you can use it to draw quilting designs—and even appliqué designs if you like—and know that they will flow beautifully around your quilt.

Example 1

You will need a basic calculator and a long tape measure to measure the exact length of the quilt borders. For our example, we will use a quilt that measures 80" x 95" *at the seam line where the borders join the quilt.* Corners are not included; they are usually treated as a separate design element. Assume that the border strips were cut 11" wide, leaving a 10"-wide design area in the border (after eliminating the inner ¼" seam allowance, the binding ¼" seam allowance, and ¼" of breathing space on each side of the border). The actual finished size of the quilt would be 101½" x 116½".

1. Double the width of the design area in the border.

    2 x 10" = 20"

NOTE: Doubling the border *width* to begin the calculations is always the first step because this measurement provides the right proportion for the repeat *length*. The resulting design will look balanced. It also gives you a starting point for determining the *exact* repeat length if the numbers don't work out to an even number of repeats.

2. Divide the border length (across the width of the quilt) by the result.
    80" ÷ 20" = 4 repeats of 20" each required for 10" x 80" border design space

3. Repeat step 2 with the remaining border length (along the length of the quilt).
    95" ÷ 20" = 4.75 repeats

    Since you must have an even number of complete repeats, you must next determine the new repeat length to fit this border.

4. Round up the result from step 3, in this case to 5 repeats.

5. To determine the required length of the repeat, divide the length of the border by the number of complete repeats required (from step 4).
    95" ÷ 5" = 19"-long repeat.

This is length of the repeat you need to fill the border—and you will need five of them. It's OK that the repeats are of different lengths for the width and length of a rectangular quilt.

Based on the math, you need to draw three different designs to create a continuous border:

1. A repeat of 20" for the shorter borders (the width of the quilt)

2. A repeat of 19" for the longer border (the length of the quilt)

3. A corner design to link the 2 borders

Example 2

Now, let's work through another example for practice.

Finished Quilt Measurement: 49½" x 61½"
Finished Quilt-Top Measurement (inside the border): 40" x 52"
Width of Border Design Area: 4"

1. Double the width of the border design area.

    2 x 4" = 8"

2. Divide the border length (across the width of the quilt) by the result.

    40" ÷ 8" = 5" repeats of 8" each for a border strip that is 4" x 40"

3. Repeat step 2 with the remaining border length (along the length of the quilt).

    52" ÷ 8" = 6.5" repeats

    In this example, the result is halfway between 6 and 7. You can use either number and divide it into 52 to get the length of a repeat.

    52" ÷ 6" repeats = 8⅜" for each repeat

    Or

    52" ÷ 7" repeats = 7³⁄₇" for each repeat

Which one should you use? I suggest drawing the spine lines for both the longer repeat and the shorter so that you can decide which is more pleasing to the eye. Does one look too steep or too stretched out? Choose the one that is most appealing to your eye. It often depends on how busy the feathers are, too.

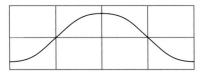

Visually Pleasing Spine Curve

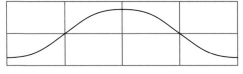

Curve Too Stretched Out

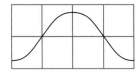

Curve Too Squished

What about odd inch increments? You will need to guesstimate fraction sizes such as ³⁄₇". For example, ³⁄₇" is very close to ⅜", so I would make my design area about ⅜" because it is easier to work in eighths than in sevenths of an inch. When I marked the border length for the repeats, I would make repeat positioning marks along the edge of the entire border and adjust the repeat length if necessary as I drew the design onto the quilt top.

Now, that math wasn't so bad, was it? Remember to draw the repeat and corner the actual size and then draw the breathing-space lines to get the actual design area. If you simply draw the design area for the corner, you will be missing the ¼" inner square where the breathing space turns the corner, and your designs will not connect.

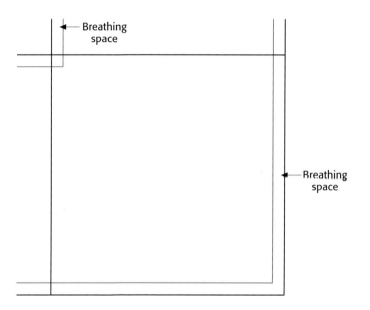

CHAPTER 6

Tapering feather designs

Now you're ready for even more interesting adventures in drawing feathers—*drawing feathers freehand*. You are past the baby steps and you can put away your coins. Drawing feathers without using coins as a crutch allows you more design freedom. You can taper the feathers at the end of the spine line to add a finishing flourish. It also allows you to fit feathers into any shape you desire.

If you have worked through the exercises so far, you will find the following exercises easier than you might think. Just remember that the basic guidelines for drawing feathers still apply.

- A feather is always half of a full heart shape.
- The starting point of the feather and the point where it touches the spine are in line and at right angles to the spine line.

Drawing a Feathered Heart—Freehand!

1. On a clean sheet of paper, draw a 15" square and breathing-space lines ¼" inside it, leaving a 14½"-square design area. Draw a line down the center of the square, dividing it in half lengthwise. You will draw and perfect feathers on one half of the square and then trace it onto the other half for the finished heart.

2. For the height line of the feathers, draw a large half-heart shape inside one of the 7¼" x 14½" design areas. Adjust the shape as needed until you are happy with the effect, being careful that the line does not extend past the lines for the breathing space at any edge. Keep the heart shape open at the top where it curves in toward the center line.

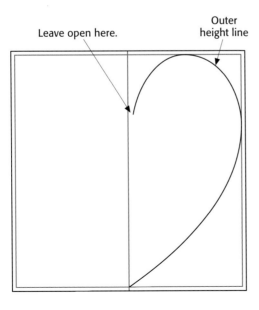

Leave open here.

Outer height line

3. Draw the spine line the desired distance from the height line. It is not necessary for this line to be equidistant from the height line, allowing you to vary the size of the feathers around the heart. For example, you can draw larger feathers at the bottom of the heart and smaller and smaller ones as you near the top—but you must plan ahead for this when you draw the spine by leaving more space between the lines at the lower point of the heart and progressively less space as you move up the shape. You can also reverse this plan, drawing smaller feathers at the bottom of the heart and larger ones nearer the top.

4. Draw the inside height line. It does not have to be the same distance from the spine either (as discussed above). At the point where the heart shape curves over at the top, try to keep the height of the inside feathers small. In this space it is difficult to draw large feathers that look balanced with the remainder of the design.

5. Refer to the illustration following step 9 for the following steps. Beginning at the bottom point of the heart, where the height line touches the center line and breathing-space line, draw half of an upside-down heart from the spine line to touch the breathing-space line. When traced to the other half of the paper, it will create a complete heart.

NOTE: I always think of feathered designs as organic and growing from a base, so I work most designs with the feathers growing up from the bottom of the design and use a heart or a teardrop as a turning point for the feathers.

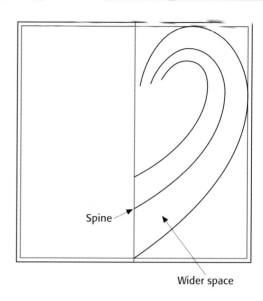

Spine

Wider space

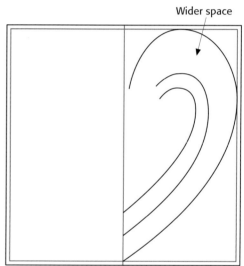

Wider space

6. Without using a coin, lightly draw curves similar to a coin top along the height line. Make the curves larger where the height line is farther away from the spine and vice versa. The result will be larger and smaller feathers. Stop drawing curves when you reach the top of the design area or just before the heart shape curves over toward the center line.

7. Complete the individual feathers, suiting each one in size and shape to the tops you have just drawn.

8. Return to the bottom point of the heart, and draw a half-teardrop shape to touch the height line on the inside of the spine line.

9. Draw curved tops for the feathers along the inside height line as described in step 6; then complete the feathers.

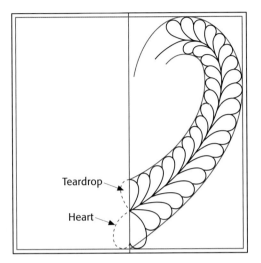

See, that wasn't all that difficult! So far so good? Don't forget that a little practice is all you need to master the technique.

FIXING YOUR FEATHERS

If your feathers seem to have lost that feather look, refer to "Avoiding Pitfalls" on page 14. What happens most often is that you lose the roundness at the beginning of the curve (coin top). Try to draw feathers as if you were still using coin tops to retain the shape, and make the center of the coin top touch the height line. Even though you may be drawing feathers much larger or much smaller than any coin top, the principles of drawing beautiful feathers remain the same.

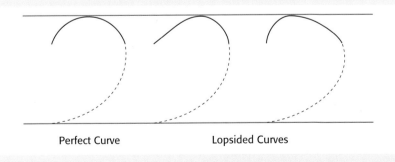

Perfect Curve   Lopsided Curves

10. To taper the feathers around the curve at the top of the heart, you must change the height and the width of the feathers in rapid progression so that they become smaller and finish neatly at the end of the spine.

At the top of the heart where you stopped drawing the feathers, draw feathers in smaller and narrower sizes in a graduating fashion on both sides of the spine. You must ignore the height lines in order to do so. The smallest and last feather should curve and appear to flow back into the spine for a finished look.

NOTE: I draw these feathers as complete feathers from the word go, but only very lightly so that I can redraw them if I don't like the look of what I have drawn. You may also wish to change the angle of the spine line as it curves back down toward the center line of the paper.

Remember to keep these feathers about ¼" away from the center line of the paper so there will be a breathing space between both halves of the heart when you have traced the completed design.

There are many ways to finish off the feathers at the end of a design; two are shown below.

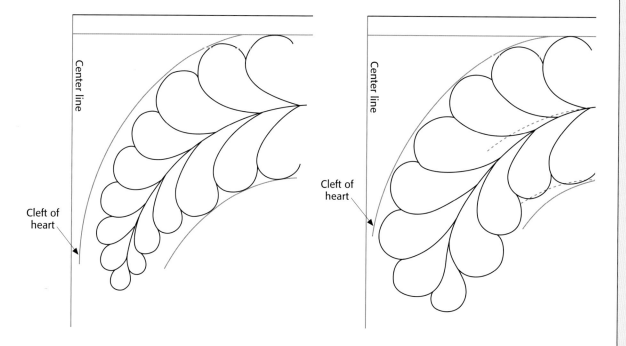

11. Check your finished design to make sure that the spacing is about the same for all feathers of a similar height. Make any adjustments to your design to finalize it.

12. Trace over the design with a dark marker. Fold the paper in half along the center line and trace the spine and feathers onto the blank half of the design area. Open the paper and follow the traced lines with a dark, permanent marker to complete your design.

Practice Project 8:
Feathered Heart Pillow or Wall Hanging

Finished Size: 17" x 17"

Crosshatched quilting in the center makes the feathered heart "pop" on the surface of this quilt or pillow top. Quilting in the outer corners echoes the curves of the outer feathers.

Materials

17" square fabric for quilted pillow-cover top or wall hanging
19" square fabric for backing
19" square of batting
18" square of fabric (if making pillow) for pillow-cover back
14"-long nylon coil zipper for closure in pillow cover
½ yard of 42"-wide fabric for hanging sleeve and binding on wall hanging

Marking the Pillow or Quilt Top

1. If you have drawn your own feathered heart design, use it for this project; otherwise use design 13 (see page 79) and enlarge 200 percent on a photocopier so that it will fit in a 15" square.

2. Transfer the feathered heart design to the center of the 17" fabric square.

Quilting and Finishing

1. Layer the quilt top with the batting and backing; pin baste the layers together.

2. Lower or disengage the feed dogs and attach the darning foot. Free-motion machine quilt the entire quilt (see "Free-Motion Machine Quilting" on page 137 and "Machine Quilting Feathers" on page 140). Remember to quilt the spine first, including the heart or teardrop. You will start and stop 4 times to quilt the feathers because all the feather quilting *begins* at the heart or teardrop.

3. To finish as a pillow cover, see page 34.

4. For a wall hanging, cut 2 strips, each 2" x 40", and 1 strip, 8" x 16" from the fabric for the binding and sleeve.

5. Bind the quilt and add a hanging sleeve and label (see page 143).

Now that you've worked through the exercise above, you are ready to learn some additional tips for tapering feathers, using any or all of the designs provided in this chapter.

1. If you prefer to trace the designs rather than draw your own, enlarge them by 200 percent on a photocopier to fit a 15" square.

2. Prepare to draw any of the designs in this chapter by drawing a 15" square on a clean sheet of paper with a 14½"-square design area inside it.

3. Draw the design of your choice in the design area and finalize it for your project.

Center line

Design 13
Enlarge 200%.

Drawing a C-Shaped Feather to Fill a Square

CURVED C-SHAPED FEATHER, *17" x 17"*

1. On a clean sheet of paper, draw a C-shaped spine line inside the 14½" design area. Add 1 or more spine lines around the C (see design 14) to fill more of the area. Draw a short spine line coming up into the center of the area from the lower curve of the C-curve.

2. Beginning at the bottom right-hand corner, draw feathers out to touch the breathing-space line around the square. The corner feathers will be extra large in order to fill the design space. Keep the inner feathers smaller than those on the outside of the design. It may help to draw a height line lightly as a guide for where to draw the inner feathers.

3. Draw feathers up the short inside spine—like a tree branch, from the bottom of the page upward. Taper all feathers to fit the areas they occupy and to finish off the ends of the spines.

NOTE: The first feathers on either side of the spine have a front—so they are more a teardrop shape or a fully enclosed shape. This gives a neat beginning to a line of feathers when they don't start against the breathing-space line with half a heart.

Design 14
Enlarge 200%.

Drawing a Square Feather Wreath

SQUARE FEATHER WREATH, *17" x 17".*

Although this is not truly a tapered design, the feathers are different sizes and fill the square design area beautifully.

1. Draw diagonal lines from point to point across the 15" square on your paper to locate the center, with a 14½"-square design area inside it. Refer to design 15 on page 84.

2. Use a compass to draw a spine line with a 5" radius and an inner height line with a radius of 2¾". Use the square breathing-space line for the outer height line. This will create a square wreath with large feathers on the outside of the spine and smaller feathers on the inside.

3. Draw a large feather across the diagonal from the breathing-space line to the spine in 1 corner only. Trace this feather onto a scrap of paper along with the breathing-space lines, spine, and diagonal line. Draw over it with a dark marker; then trace this feather into each of the 3 remaining corners on your design sheet, using all the lines to position it.

4. Draw feathers along the spine between the corner feathers on one side of the square only. Trace these feathers and the spine onto another scrap of paper, darken, and trace onto the other 3 sides of the square, just as you did the corner feathers. This way the larger outside feathers will be uniform around the entire wreath.

5. Draw the inner feathers as you would for a circular feathered wreath (see page 26).

Design 15
Enlarge 200%.

Drawing Long Feathers to Fill a Triangle

LONG FEATHERS TO FILL A TRIANGLE, *17" x 17".*

Two feathered triangles fill a square beautifully. Similar feathers can be drawn to fill a diamond shape as in "Pine Burr" on page 7.

1. Divide the 15" square on your paper in half diagonally. Draw ¼"-wide breathing-space lines inside 1 triangle on all sides.

2. Draw a slightly curved spine line in the center of the triangular design area. The height lines for the feathers are the lines for the breathing space.

3. Begin drawing feathers according to the rules you have learned from previous exercises.

4. After completing the first few feathers, you must change your technique a bit. Even though there is room for feathers with larger (wider) feather tops because there is more room (height) between the spine and the breathing space lines, keep the feather tops about the same size from here until you near the end of the spine. Make the remaining feathers smaller and smaller, following the normal rules again.

    When completing these longer feathers, ignore the rule for keeping the beginning of the feather and the bottom of the feather where it touches the spine at right angles to the spine line. Instead, curve the feather so that it is pleasing to the eye. This might sound a bit vague, but study design 16 to see how a rounder curve makes the feathers flow while still fitting in with the smaller, normally drawn feathers.

5. When you are happy with your feathered triangle design, trace over it with a dark marking pen.

6. Fold the square in half on the center diagonal and trace the design into the remaining half of the square. Or, trace the completed design onto another piece of paper, reverse it, and tape it to the first design to complete the square.

NOTE: When quilting these long, narrow feathers, refer to "Machine Quilting Long, Thin Feathers" on page 140. Remember to count back from the corner feather to have a single line of quilting over the top outside edge of this major feather. Work out ahead of time where the double line quilting will be.

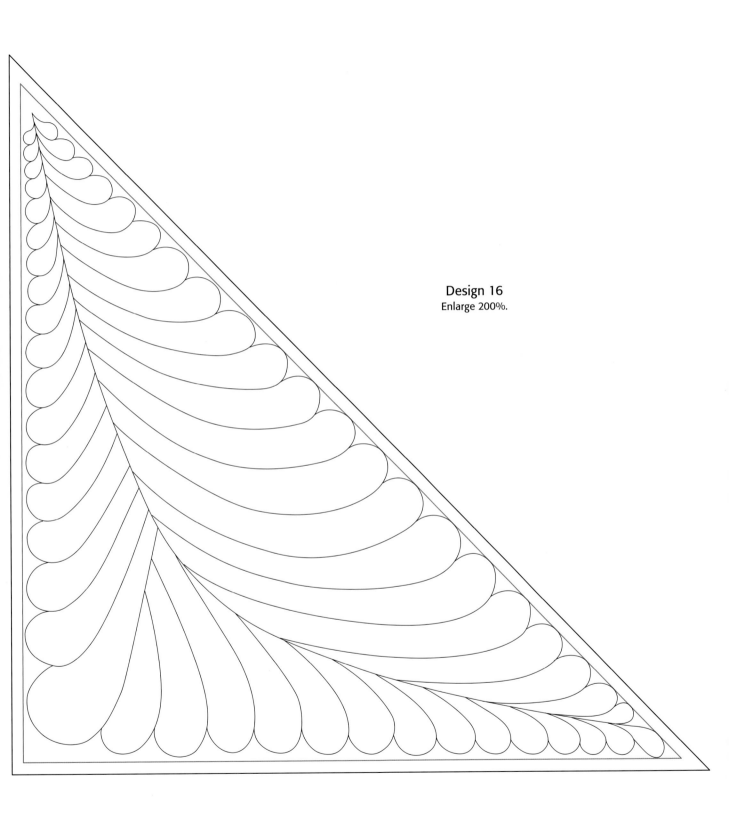

Design 16
Enlarge 200%.

CHAPTER 7

Border feather variations

In this chapter you will learn how to alter the appearance of border designs by varying the height of the feathers along a spine line or by altering the spine line itself.

Drawing Border Feathers from a Corner

You will use hearts and/or teardrops as turning points in a design that connects the corner design with the border design. The feathers flow out *from* the corner in both directions and generally finish in the center of the border strip. This is *not* a continuous border design.

For this example, we will use a border width of 4" surrounding a 16" square. In the center, you can trace and quilt any of the designs that we have worked with so far that fit a 15" square.

1. Draw half the border length and the corner area together as one design area; in this case, a rectangle that is 4" x 12" (the 4" corner square plus ½ of the 16"- long border). Lightly draw the outline of the corner so that you don't forget you have combined the border and the corner together (different from previous exercises).

2. Draw a diagonal line from the inside corner to the outside corner of the border corner and draw breathing-space lines as shown below.

3. If the border is fairly short, draw a freehand curve for the spine from the diagonal line, along the border length. For long borders, determine the correct repeat length as directed in "The Math of Repeats," beginning on page 70.

4. Draw height lines on each side of the spine line.

5. At the outer corner of the border corner section, draw a half heart (a) (see page 90) on the diagonal line so that it touches the spine and the breathing-space lines.

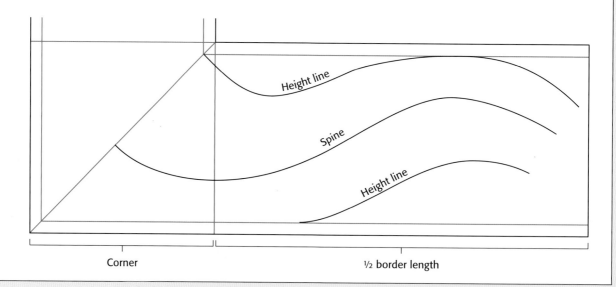

Corner   ½ border length

6. Draw freehand feathers along the spine working from the heart until you almost reach the end of the spine.

7. Go back to the inner corner, draw a half teardrop (b) with the point touching the point of the half-heart shape and the full curve of the shape touching the inner square for the breathing space.

8. Draw freehand feathers along the inside of the spine line, working from the teardrop until you almost reach the end of the spine.

9. Draw tapered feathers (see "Drawing a Feathered Heart—Freehand!" on page 73) on both sides of the spine with the last one ending ¼" from the end of the rectangle. This allows for a small space between the 2 border designs where they meet at the center of the border.

10. When you are pleased with your drawing, trace over the lines with a dark marker.

11. Fold the paper along the diagonal line and trace the design into the remaining half of the corner space to finish your border design.

(a)

(b)

Design 17
Enlarge 125%.

Practice Project 9:
Pillow Cover with Feathers from a Corner

Finished Pillow Size: 24½" x 24½"

If you examine this photo closely, you will see that there are 2 different border patterns, one in which the feathers fill the design area and the other in which the feathers follow a curved height line. The center feathers are different designs also. Here, a variation in the width of the feather tops creates a different look in each triangular design area.

Materials

Yardage is based on 42"-wide fabric, with 40" of usable width after preshrinking.

1⅝ yds. of 42"-wide fabric for the pillow top and back★
28" square of backing fabric
28" square of batting
22"-long nylon coil zipper

★If you prefer to make a wall hanging, you will need only 1 yd. of 42"-wide fabric, which includes enough for a hanging sleeve and the binding.

Cutting and Marking the Pillow Cover Top

1. From the pillow cover (or wall hanging) fabric, cut a 26" square. If you are making a pillow, cut a 28" square from the remaining fabric for the pillow cover back and set aside.

2. If you plan to use design 17 (page 90) rather than draw your own version first, enlarge it on a photocopier by 133 percent to make it fit a 4" x 12" rectangle.

3. Draw a 24" square in the center of the 26" square. Draw a 16" square and a 15" square inside the first, centering each one. Add a line ¼" outside the 24" square for positioning the binding.

4. Transfer one of the 15" square feathered designs that you have already drawn into the center square (see "Transferring Quilting Designs" on page 136).

5. Transfer design 17 into the borders and corners.

Quilting and Finishing

1. Layer the pillow top (or quilt top) with the batting and backing squares; pin baste the layers together.

2. Attach the walking foot or engage the even-feed feature on your machine. Quilt all straight lines first.

3. Drop or disengage the feed dogs and attach the darning foot. Free-motion quilt the feather spines first, followed by the feathers (see "Free-Motion Machine Quilting" on page 137 and "Machine Quilting Feathers" on page 140).

4. To finish the pillow cover, cut a 4" x 28" strip from the 28" square for the pillow cover back and construct the cover as directed on page 34. Baste the pieces together in the center 22" of the seam when you sew the pieces together.

5. To make the square into a wall hanging, cut an 8" x 23" strip from the 42"-wide fabric for the hanging sleeve and 3 strips, each 2" x 40", for the binding.

6. Bind the quilt and add a hanging sleeve and label.

Drawing Deep Repeat Border Curves

You can draw deep repeat curves or spines by altering the starting point of the spine line. The manner of determining the repeat length remains the same as discussed in "The Math of Repeats" on page 70.

The feathers use the breathing-space line as the height line and look lovely as fairly narrow border designs, or in a larger border with other designs at either side to fill the design area (see the "Old English Tulips" quilts in the gallery on pages 124–128).

In this type of curve, you disregard the rules you've learned as you draw the feathers. Drawing the corner also requires a different approach.

In the following example, you will draw a design for a 3"-wide finished border to surround an 18" center square. To determine the number of repeats required, apply the formula you learned in "The Math of Repeats," beginning on page 70.

- 2 x the border width = length of border repeat if it is a whole number

  2 x 3" = 6"-long border repeat

- border length ÷ repeat length = number of repeats

  18" ÷ 6" = 3 repeats of 6" each

NOTE: Here I have taken the actual width of the border (3") and not taken off ¼" for breathing spaces, because it simplifies the math.

1. Draw a repeat length 3" x 6" and draw lines for the breathing space ¼" inside each of the long edges of the rectangle.

2. Refer to step 3 in "Curved Border Repeats" on page 44 to divide the rectangle into sections. The curve for the spine this time begins at the breathing-space line in the lower left section and curves to the top right-hand corner of the same section.

3. Trace off this section with the curve, turn it 180°, and place the tracing under the drawing. Trace the curve onto the second top left section.

4. Fold the paper in half at the center line and trace the curve onto the remaining half of the rectangle. The result is a steeply curved repeat with 2 half bottom curves and 1 full top curve.

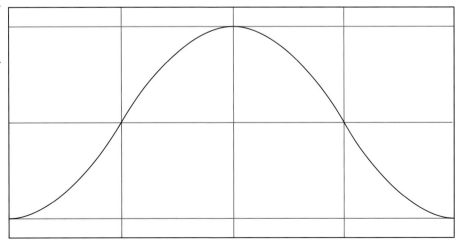

5. Study the next illustration. Notice that the feathers are not all the same size. They are smallest where the distance from the breathing-space line to the spine is short and they get progressively larger where the curve of the spine deepens.

Draw the first feather following the normal "rules." Distribute the next feathers evenly throughout this deep curve. Lightly draw the tops of the feathers along the breathing-space line (height line in this case), making them roughly the same size. Draw the feathers; they will curve farther than they would if you were following the rules and are similar to "Drawing Long Feathers to Fill a Triangle" (page 85). Note that the last of these feathers should flow into the curve of the spine (the second farthest feather to the right in the illustration). The last small feather to the right of the design may be left off; it depends on the amount of space left in the curve. You may need to redraw the tops of the feathers so that they fit inside the available space.

Fold here to trace the second half into this section.

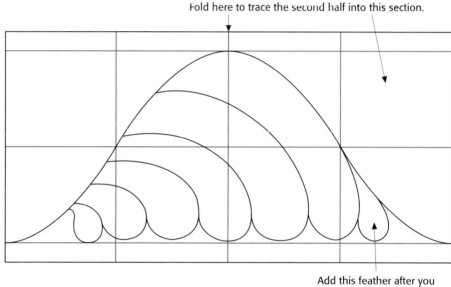

Add this feather after you are pleased with the positioning of the others.

6. To create the border pattern using this repeat, you will need to bend the rules again. It is impossible to draw the feathers into the bottom half curve because the feathers curve across the repeat line. Instead, you must draw a half repeat next to the bottom curve. In fact, you draw 1½ repeats to be able to draw the feathers. Look carefully at design 18 on the next page.

Trace the feathers from the full top curve onto a separate piece of paper and flip it over so that the feathers flow in the same direction as those in the full upper curve—they're just upside down now.

Trace the feathers into the bottom curve. Note that the feathers are the same in both curves. It's really quite simple!

NOTE: When I transfer these border repeats onto the quilt top, I make marks on the top where the repeats will be to make sure I am lining them up correctly and to make sure I don't get confused. There is potential for confusion because I had to draw 1½ repeats in order to draw feathers on both sides of the spine line.

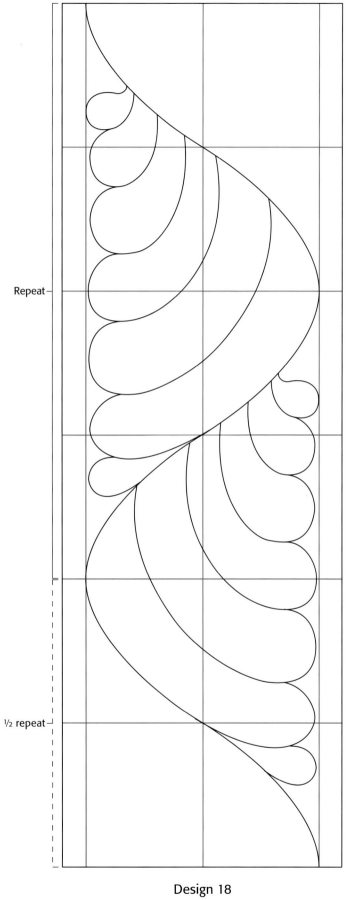

Repeat

½ repeat

Design 18

Drawing Corners for Deep Repeat Border Curves

To create feathers that flow around the corner, you will need to draw more than just the corner square. That's because the corner feathers carry on into a half curve of the repeat at each side of the corner. In the example, the repeat enters and leaves the corner at the outer edge of the quilt. Study the illustrations below and on page 97.

1. Draw the corner as a 3" x 3" square and add a 3" square (½ of a repeat) at each inner edge of the square. Draw the lines for ¼" breathing spaces as shown.

2. Draw the curve for the spine around the corner.

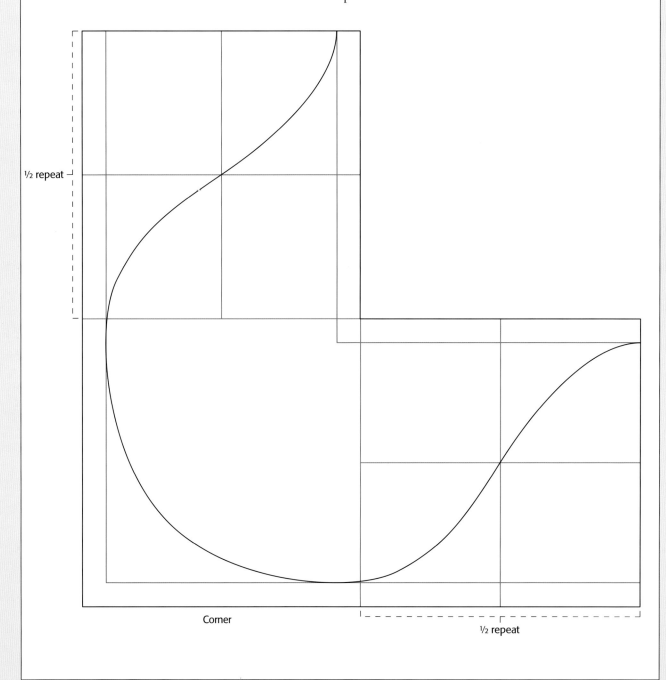

½ repeat

Corner

½ repeat

3. Fill in feathers similar to the feathers of the repeat curve, making sure that the feathers flow in the same direction as the repeat feathers.

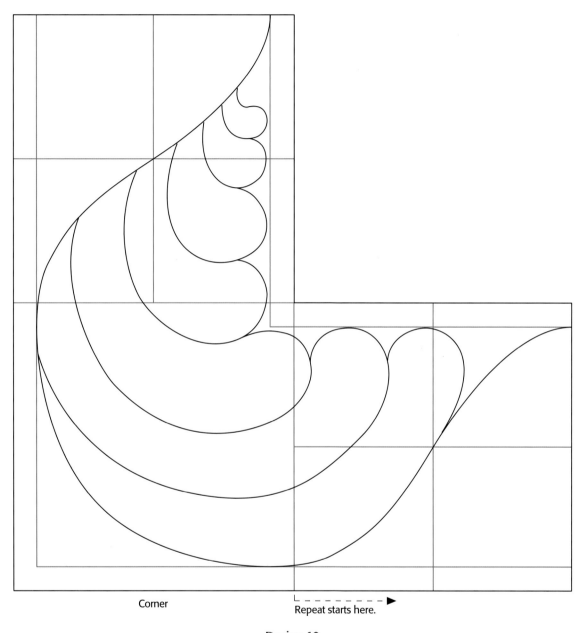

Corner

Repeat starts here. ▶

Design 19

Drawing a Deep Curved Border Variation

Another lovely border design with deep curves has a spine line that begins slightly away from the breathing-space line and is drawn in a similar manner to the one described above. The space between the spine line and the breathing-space line is dependent on the border width.

    With this spine line, smaller feathers are drawn right up to the start and finish of the repeat so that they will be continuous when the repeats are drawn onto the quilt. The large feathers are drawn in the same manner as for the design above and the smaller feathers still obey the "rules" and must be contained within and touch each end of the repeat length.

Here again you need to draw 1½ repeats to draw the feathers on both sides of the spine line.

    To create the corner, follow the same procedure, remembering that the small feathers should flow continuously around the outer edge of the corner, just touching the breathing space, and should be contained within the corner design area.

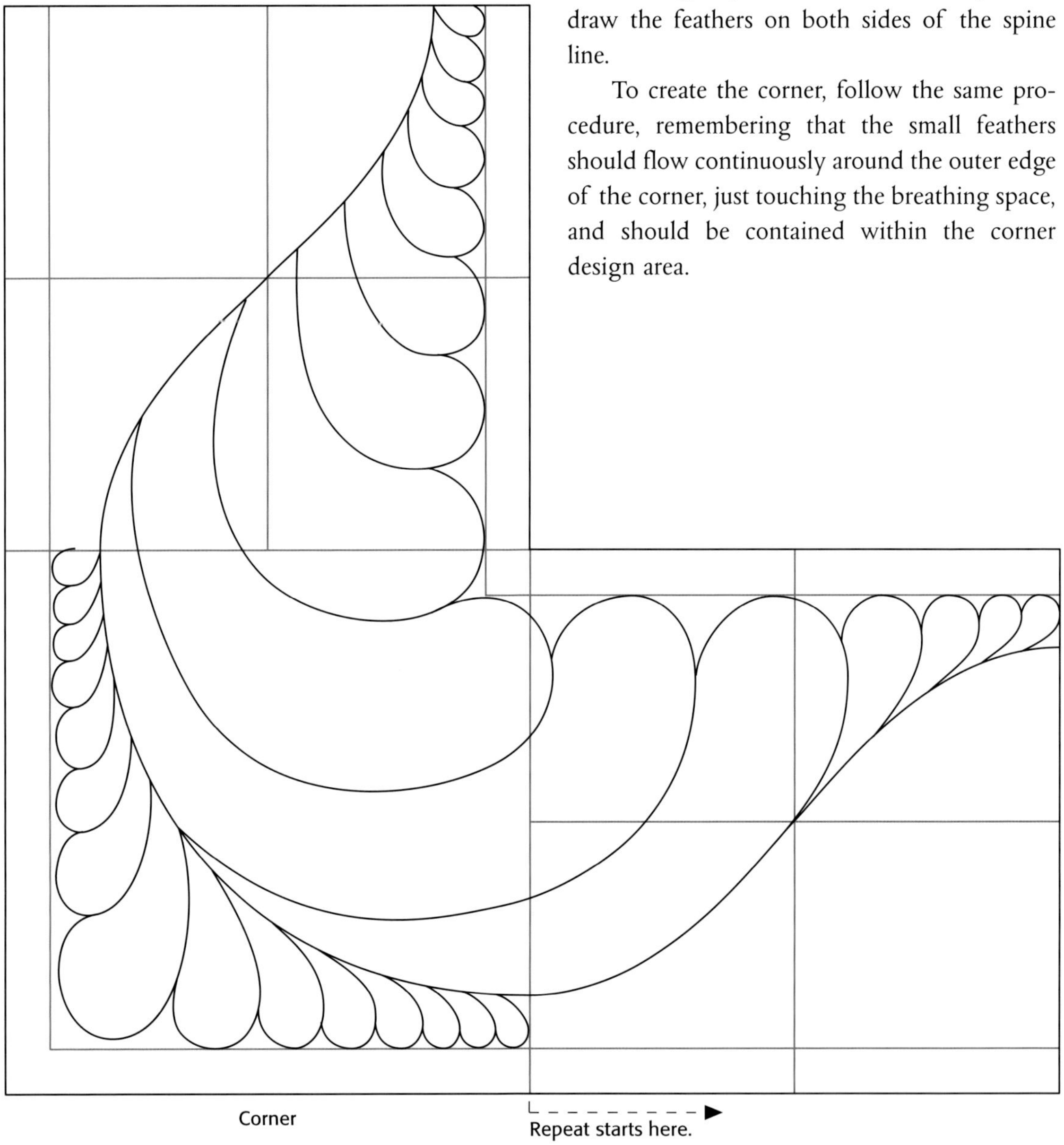

Corner

Repeat starts here.

Design 21

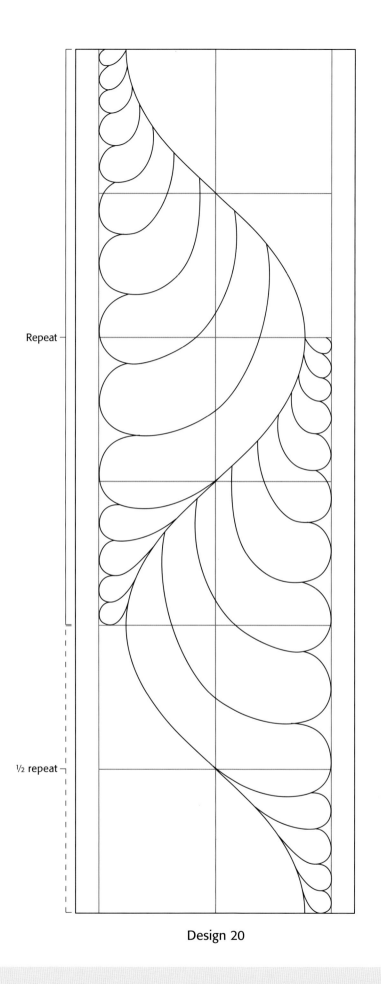

Repeat

½ repeat

Design 20

Practice Project 10: Wall Hanging with Deep Repeat Curves

WALL HANGING WITH DEEP REPEAT CURVES 1, *24½" x 24½".*
In this small quilt, the curve for the spine in the border begins at the breathing space line and the feathers are contained within each curve.

WALL HANGING WITH DEEP REPEAT CURVES 2, *24½" x 24½".*
In this quilt, the curve of the spine begins slightly away from the breathing-space line and the feathers flow continuously around the border.

Materials

Yardage is based on 42"-wide fabric, with 40" of usable width after preshrinking.

26" square of fabric for quilt top
28" square of fabric for backing
½ yd. of fabric for the binding and hanging sleeve
28" square of batting

Marking the Quilt Top

1. Draw a 24" square in the center of the 26" fabric square. Draw an 18" square and a 15" square inside the first, centering each one. Add a line ¼" outside the 24" square for positioning the binding.

2. Transfer the 15" feathered design of your choice into the center.

3. Decide on a background design to fill in the area from the design inside the 15" square to the 18" square or draw 3 straight quilting lines inside the 18" square, spacing them ½" apart. If you want to quilt a grid anywhere on your quilt top, draw it now (see page 32).

4. Use designs 18 and 19 or designs 20 and 21 for the borders and corners and transfer to the quilt top—or use your own designs.

Quilting and Finishing

1. Layer the quilt top with batting and backing; pin baste the layers together.

2. Attach the walking foot or engage the even-feed feature on your machine. Quilt straight lines first, but do not quilt the grid until you have finished quilting the feathers.

3. Drop or disengage the feed dogs and attach the darning foot. Free-motion quilt the feather spines and then the feathers (see "Free-Motion Machine Quilting" on page 137 and "Machine Quilting Feathers" on page 140). Quilt the border feathers in the manner described for long, narrow feathers on page 140.

4. Quilt the background fill that you've chosen, switching back to the walking foot if it is a straight-line pattern such as a grid.

5. From the binding fabric, cut 1 strip, 8" x 24", for the hanging sleeve, and 3 strips, each 2" x 40", for the binding.

6. Bind the quilt and add a hanging sleeve and label (see pages 142–143).

Drawing a Border of Feathered Swirls or Curls

This border design uses a repeat length determined like any other (see "The Math of Repeats" on page 70), but within the repeat length the spine line is very different.

1. Draw a repeat 6½" x 10½" and draw ¼"-wide breathing spaces inside the 2 long edges. Draw lines that divide the repeat in half lengthwise and crosswise.

2. Draw a 6½" x 6½" corner and draw the breathing-space lines. Divide in half with a diagonal line.

3. For the outer height line of the feathers for the corner, draw an urn shape with the curved end touching the breathing-space lines at the outer corner of the square. Add the spine and inner height lines where desired.

4. Draw feathers around the spine on both sides of the line, keeping them contained within the corner design area.

Design 22

5. Place the repeat length next to the corner square and make dots at the points where the corner spine will enter the repeat. This is your guide for positioning the spine and height lines of the repeat.

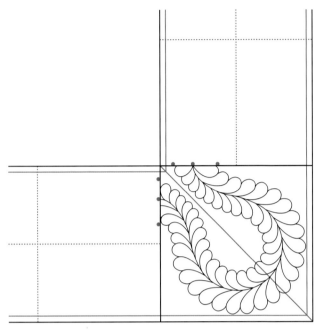

Marking Dots for the Repeat Placement of the Spine

6. If you wish, you can draw a curved feathered border repeat as drawn in chapter 3 (beginning on page 44) and link that with this corner. Try design 23. In this design, feathered swirls curl away from each other in opposite directions, each one filling a half repeat. They are linked at the center of the repeat and also have a small "branch" that links them with the next repeat.

NOTE: Do not use a compass to draw the spine—the curl is softer than a true circular arc.

Because the angle in a repeat swirl is so steep, you will find it necessary to redraw the "branch" angle of the spine somewhat when connecting the last border repeat on the left end of the border to the corner for a smooth flow. Draw new feathers to fit into the area.

Redraw spine to make
a smooth curve
where it joins the corner.

Design 23
Enlarge 125%.

Practice Project 11: Blue Whole-Cloth Quilt

Finished Size: 34½" x 34½"

In this one small quilt you'll find a variety of lovely feather quilting designs—a feather wreath, a straight-spine feather continuous border, and continuous feather swirls in the border. Another quilt that features similar swirl quilting designs is "Apricot Table Runner" on page 131 in the gallery.

Materials

Yardage is based on 42"-wide fabric, with 40" of usable width after preshrinking.

1½ yds. blue fabric for quilt top, hanging sleeve, and binding
38" square of fabric for the backing
38" x 38" square of batting

Cutting and Marking the Quilt Top

1. From the blue fabric, cut:
    1 square, 36" x 36"
    1 strip, 8" x 34", for hanging sleeve
    4 strips, 2" x 40", for binding

2. Draw a 34" square in the center of the blue fabric square. Center a 21" and then a 15" square inside it. Add ¼" drawn lines outside the 34" square for positioning the binding.

3. Choose a feathered design for a 15" square from those in this book or one that you have drawn, and transfer it to the center of the fabric square.

4. Transfer the 3" straight-spine feather design 1 on page 21 into the area between the lines for the 21" and 15" squares. Repeat to fit the length, leaving the 3" x 3" corners unmarked for the corner design provided below, design 24, or draw your own corner to make this border a continuous straight-spine feather border. Check that all your feathers are flowing in the same direction.

Design 24

5. For a 1" diagonal grid behind the central feathers (optional), draw dots 1" apart on all sides of the 15" square. Beginning at a corner, join the dots and extend the lines out to touch the straight-spine feathers. See "Masking an Accurate Quilting Grid," page 32.

6. Transfer corner design 22 into the outer corners and repeat swirls (design 23) into the outer borders. Alter the feathers as needed where the border feather repeat leads into the left corner from the last swirl. Make sure that your border designs are all positioned correctly so that they flow in one continuous line around the border. (It's easy to flip a piece and trace a section upside down.)

Quilting and Finishing

1. Layer the quilt top with batting and backing; pin baste the layers together.

2. Attach the walking foot or engage the even-feed feature on your machine and quilt all the straight lines except the grid—the spine of the straight-spine feather border and the line dividing the straight feather border from the swirl border. Do not quilt the 15"-square lines as the grid will cut across them.

3. Attach the darning foot and free-motion quilt the feather spines that are not already quilted (the straight-spine feather), followed by the feathers (see pages 137 and 140).

NOTE: I suggest working from the outside of the quilt into the center on a whole-cloth quilt *after* doing all the straight lines. This flattens the area at the outer edge of the quilt and allows you to remove the pins so that the work is less bulky and easier to handle as you move to the center. It also means you will have "warmed up" your free-motion machine-quilting technique and will be less likely to make small errors in your stitching in the center of the quilt. Since the quilt center is the focal point, errors are more likely to be noticed there.

4. Raise the feed dogs and replace the walking foot. Quilt the straight-line grid in the background.

5. Bind the quilt and add a hanging sleeve and label (see pages 142–143).

CHAPTER 8

Open feathers

Until now you have been drawing feathers and perfecting your machine-quilting skills with the traditional or overlapping feathers used by hand quilters for centuries. This chapter addresses open feathers, the ones used by machine quilters because they are so easy to stitch. Knowing how to do both types of feathers offers you many more choices. What you draw ultimately depends on how you want your finished quilt to look.

Open feathers are very simple feathers to quilt by machine. They are all separate feathers (no double-line quilting) and can be quilted without regard to the flow or direction of the feathers. And, there are no spine lines.

So, why do you learn to do them at the end of the book? I believe you will be able to draw and quilt these feathers and the ones in the following chapter much more easily if you first understand how traditional feathers are drawn and stitched following the basic rules.

Drawing Straight-Spine Open Feathers

To begin, we'll go back to using coins.

1. Draw a 4" x 8" rectangle with breathing-space lines inside each long edge.

2. Draw the spine halfway between these as a guide only. You will *not* quilt the spine.

3. Draw large coin tops along the height lines (which are also the breathing-space lines), but leave a small gap between each coin top rather than draw them to touch each other according to the traditional rules.

4. Beginning with the second coin top (we will return to the first coin top later), curve the feather to a point that is below the end of the coin top of the first one. Leave a small gap between the end of this curve and the spine line; they shouldn't touch. The resulting feather will be a much longer curve than for a traditional straight-spine feather.

5. Complete the curves for the next feathers in the same way; then go back and finish drawing the first feather. Make the same curve for this feather, realizing that a small portion will be outside the rectangle.

6. To finish each feather, draw a line from where you completed its curve near the spine line up to join the next coin top, following the shape but not on top of the curve of the feather in front. Keep these feathers voluptuous (fat and curvy) and check that the curves do not touch the spine line.

7. Draw the feathers on the other side of the spine line in the same manner. There must be space between the rows of feathers to create the illusion of a spine.

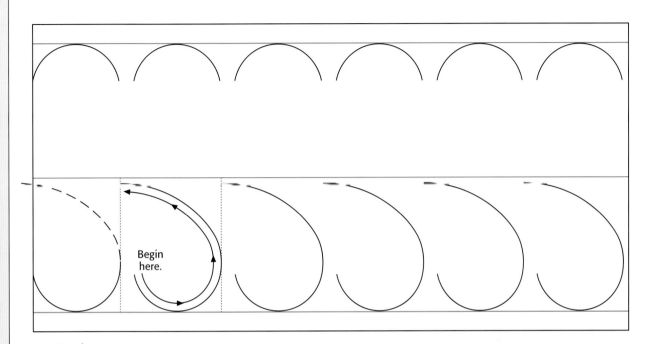

Begin here.

Complete feather 1 last.

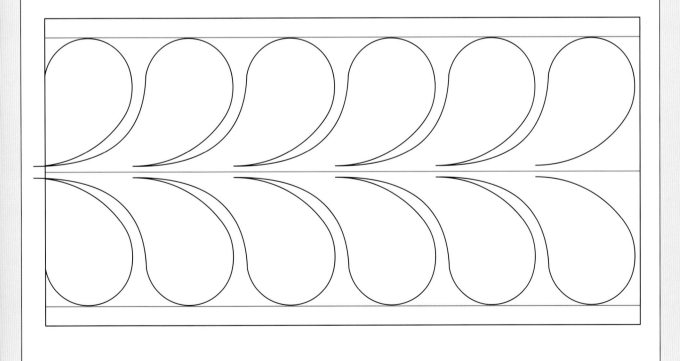

Drawing an Open-Feather Wreath

1. Refer to design 25 on the facing page. Draw a 15" square and draw breathing-space lines inside the square.

2. Locate the center of the square by drawing lines from corner to corner and mark the point with a dark dot.

3. Using a compass, draw circles for the spine and height lines with radii of 7¼", 5", and 2¾".

4. Using a large coin, draw coin tops around the height lines, remembering to leave a small gap between each one. They should all be approximately the same size and finish with a full coin top.

5. Draw open feathers as described for straight-spine open feathers on page 108. Remember that because you are drawing around a circle, the spot where the curve of the feather nearly touches the spine line is related to the compass point and the end of the coin top of the previous feather. (This is different from drawing traditional feathers because of the space between coin tops.) The inside feathers can have quite long curves, depending on the distance between coin tops. The greater the distance, the longer the curves.

Drawing an Open-Feather Heart

1. Refer to design 26 on page 112. Draw a half-heart shape with height lines and breathing space inside a 15" square as directed on pages 73–74 in chapter 6, "Tapering Feather Designs."

2. This time, freehand draw the coin-top shapes, leaving a small gap between each one, so you can make these open feathers. Remember the spine line is only a guide and the feathers do not touch it.

3. Draw the feathers, tapering them where the heart curls back toward the center. When you are happy with the appearance of the completed half-heart quilting design, fold the paper and trace it onto the other half of the square.

Design 25
Enlarge 200%.

Design 26
Enlarge 200%.

Practice Projects 12 and 13: Open-Feather Wall Hangings

OPEN-FEATHER WREATH,
15½" x 15½". The grid in the center of this wreath flatters and defines the open feathers. For another quilt with open-feather designs, see "Blue Open Feathers" on page 135 in the gallery.

OPEN-FEATHER HEART,
15½" x 15½". The feathers in this design are even more prominent because I used a 30-weight variegated thread. Playing with thread color and type opens another world of creativity in quilting.

Materials for 1 Wallhanging

⅝ yard fabric for the quilt top, hanging sleeve, and binding
19" square of fabric for the backing
19" square of batting

Cutting and Marking the Quilt Top

1. From the fabric for the quilt top, hanging sleeve, and binding, cut:
    1 square, 17" x 17"
    1 strip, 8" x 15"
    2 strips, 2" x 40"

2. Enlarge design 25 or 26 (pages 111 and 112) by 200 percent on a photocopier to make them fit a 15" square—or use your own 15" designs.

3. Draw a 15" square in the center of the 17" quilt top and transfer the desired design to the center. Draw a line ¼" outside the 15" square for positioning the binding.

4. **Optional:** Draw a grid (see page 32) to quilt in the center of the design.

Quilting and Finishing

1. Layer the quilt top with batting and backing; pin baste the layers together.

2. Lower or disengage the feed dogs and attach the darning foot. Free-motion quilt the open-feather design (see "Free-Motion Machine Quilting" on page 137 and "Machine Quilting Feathers" on page 140).

3. Quilt the background inside the heart or wreath. If your design is a grid, raise the feed dogs and change to the walking foot. Otherwise, free-motion quilt the background design of your choice.

4. Bind the quilt and add a hanging sleeve and label (see pages 142–143).

Project 14: Sampler Quilt

Here's an excellent opportunity to showcase what you've learned by working through the exercises in this workbook. Use the block patterns in the book—or better yet the designs you've drawn yourself as you've learned to draw feathered quilting designs.

Finished Size: 60½" x 60½"

Look closely and you will see that this quilt includes many of the block designs featured in Feathers That Fly. *A straight-spine feather quilting design straddles the seam lines between the blocks for block dividers, and the border is awash in lovely deep feather curves that draw your eye around the finished quilt.*

Materials

Yardage is based on 42"-wide fabric, with 40" of usable width after preshrinking.

¾ yd. fabric for border
9 different solid-colored 18½" squares for the blocks
3⅔ yds. fabric for backing
½ yd. fabric for binding
64" x 64" piece of batting

Piecing the Quilt Top

1. Arrange the 9 quilt squares in 3 rows of 3 blocks each and sew together in rows. Press the seams in opposite directions from row to row. Sew the rows together and press the seams in one direction.

2. From the border fabric, cut 6 strips, each 4" x 40". Cut a 22"-long and a 16"-long piece from each of 2 of these strips. Sew one of these shorter strips to each of the remaining 4 strips. Trim the shorter pieced strips to 54½" and the longer pieced strips to 60½".

3. Sew the 2 shorter strips to 2 opposite sides of the quilt top and press the seams toward the borders. Sew the longer border strips to the top and bottom edges of the quilt top. Press toward the borders.

Marking the Quilt Top

1. Choose 9 feather block designs from the 10 different 15" block designs given in this book and transfer them to the centers of the 9 squares.

2. Transfer the straight-spine feathers design 1 (page 21), centering it over the seam lines between blocks, using the seam line as the spine. The straight feathers form a sort of "sashing" between the blocks.

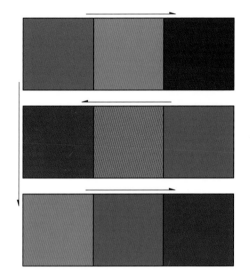

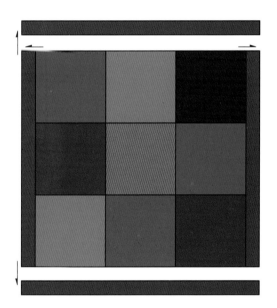

3. Draw only one side of the straight-spine feather at the outer edge of the quilt top, using the border seam as the spine with feathers in the blocks.

4. For the border, choose designs 18 and 19 on pages 95 and 97 or designs 20 and 21 on pages 98–99. Each of these is a 6" repeat, so you will trace the chosen design 9 times on each side of the quilt top and the corner design 4 times.

Quilting and Finishing

1. From the backing fabric, cut 2 pieces of equal length (cut in half crosswise). Sew the 2 pieces together with a ¼"-wide seam and trim to make a 64" x 64" square.

2. Layer the quilt top with batting and backing; pin baste the layers together.

3. Attach the walking foot or engage the even-feed feature on your machine and quilt all straight lines in the design.

4. Lower or disengage the feed dogs and attach the darning foot. Free-motion quilt all the feather designs, remembering to quilt the spines first before the feathers themselves (see "Free-Motion Machine Quilting" on page 137 and "Machine Quilting Feathers" on page 140).

5. Attach the walking foot to quilt any grids in your design.

6. Bind the quilt and add a hanging sleeve and label (see pages 142–143).

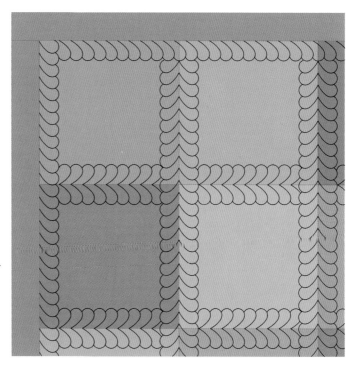

CHAPTER 9

Fast and free feathers

I have Caryl Breyer Fallert to thank for showing me how to quilt these feathers. These are the quickest and easiest feathers of all because there is *no* drawing involved. "What," I hear you say, "no drawing?" The answer is simple. I believe it is easier to attempt these feathers after you have had practice drawing and stitching traditional feather shapes and you know the "rules."

These feathers are wonderful for stitching with the professional long-arm quilting machines. I do not pretend to know a lot about these machines, having only used them a few times, but I feel that Caryl's technique of completing the feathers with one pass of the machine makes sense for these machines, too. The possible variations are limited only by your imagination and willingness to experiment.

Since these feathers are not drawn on the fabric, there is no printed pattern for the design—that's one of the reasons they are quick. Included here is a photo of one of my first attempts at this process so that you can better understand the steps involved.

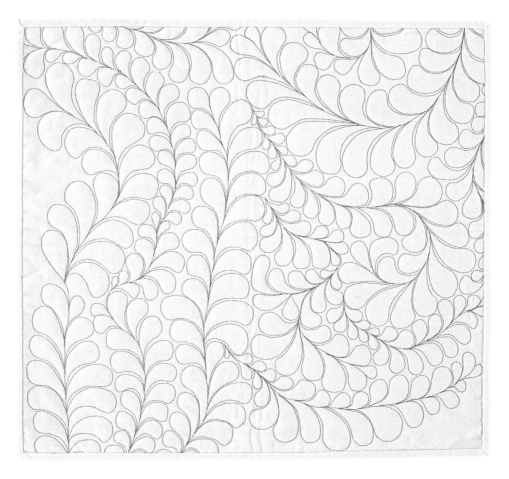

FAST AND FREE FEATHERS, *18" x 20"*.
Thread in a contrasting color makes the feathers more distinct in this small wall hanging.

Exercise 1: Drawing Straight-Spine Fast and Free Feathers

We'll use paper for the following exercise so that you'll have some sense of how to proceed when you actually try stitching one of these feathered designs—*without* drawing a pattern on the fabric. The numbers in the illustration below and on the facing page indicate the order in which the feathers are drawn along the spine line. They do not correspond to the numbered steps.

1. Draw a faint line for the spine on the paper as a guide for where you want the feathers to go. When you get used to the movement, you'll be able to omit this line entirely. Start at the bottom of the page and work your way up the page.

2. With your pencil, draw feather 1 by curving out to the left in a shape similar to an open feather (as discussed in the previous chapter). Draw from the spine line and back again to the spine line to touch the point where you started. Always draw the curve closest to yourself or the bottom of the paper first.

3. Curve out to the right and back again in an open-feather shape, this time touching the first feather as you curve back to the spine line at a point above the place where feather 1 begins and ends. Keep the pencil on the paper all the time and you'll find that you quickly build up a rhythm of drawing these feathers—and they're fun to draw. Remember to draw the curve closest to yourself first and then complete the feather.

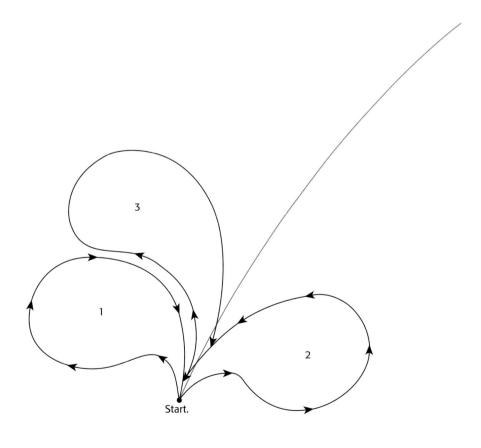

4. Continue drawing open feathers to the left and right of the spine in this manner, always bringing your pencil back to touch the preceding feather higher up than where you started to keep a continuous flow of feathers and to build up a smooth spine line. If you don't keep the spine smooth, these feathers will look messy.

5. Continue up the spine line you have drawn, keeping the feathers a similar shape and size, until you are nearly to the end. Then start tapering the feathers, making them smaller and smaller in shape and size to finish with a single feather at the end of the spine.

Now that was easy, wasn't it?

Exercise 2: Drawing Curved-Spine Fast and Free Feathers

To begin, lightly draw a curved spine line and follow the steps on pages 119–120. Instead of always drawing each new feather on the other side of the spine from the one just completed, draw two feathers on the outside of the spine where it begins to curve (feathers 5 and 6 in the illustration). These two will be on the same side of the spine. Then alternate feathers until you need to curve again (as for feathers 12, 13, 17, and 18).

Draw a curved spine line on paper and practice drawing feathers in this manner until you are ready to try stitching one. Drawing feathers on paper trains your eye and hand to work together; then you can transfer that skill to the sewing machine.

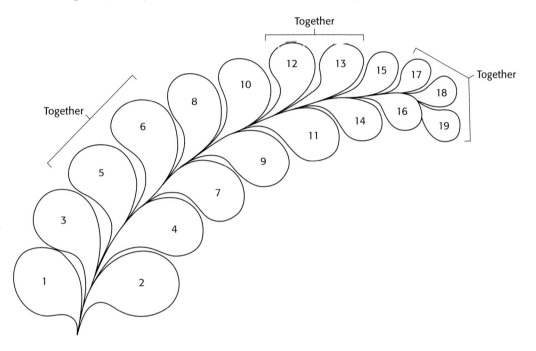

When you are ready to try your hand at stitching your own fast and free feathers on fabric, use a fairly fast stitching speed and the feathers will flow more smoothly. Don't forget to leave enough room for breathing space around the feathers so that they don't look squashed inside a design area.

A Final Word

If you've worked through the exercises in this book, it's time for a pat on the back. Go back and look at your drawing and stitching samples to see the progress you've made as you've perfected your feather stitching skills. I hope you've had fun and that all your "feathers fly" in perfect formation as you use them to create stunning quilts.

Gallery of Quilts

CHAIN AND STARS, *62" x 64".*

Chains of red surround pinwheel stars in this graphic quilt. Four quilting designs were used to create the border pattern, which flows from the corner turning points to the halfway point in each border. Trapunto quilting across the quilt surface hides the piecing lines.

BLUE FEATHERED STARS II, *83" x 83".*
Purchased stencils were used for the feathered quilting designs in this striking quilt that features pieced feathered star blocks surrounded by an appliquéd border. Using the principles discussed in "The Math of Repeats" beginning on page 70, I created a continuous curved border and corner design for the appliqué.

  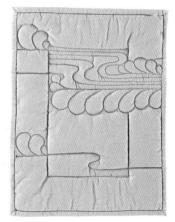

TRIPTYCH, *each 9" x 12". Feather quilting defines the linear design in these three small quilted pieces.*

It should be obvious, by now, that the quilting pattern you choose has a dramatic visual effect on a quilt's overall composition. The five quilts that follow are very good examples. All were pieced using the same block pattern and fabric, the same batting and the same backing. The difference is in the quilting patterns used from quilt to

OLD ENGLISH TULIPS I,

61" x 63". The diagonal quilted grid across the piecing is a much-loved traditional quilting method. The traditional feather border design composed of two repeats on each border strip turns each corner in a horseshoe shape so that there is a continuous flow of feather designs around the quilt.

quilt. This is the same technique I used in my first book, *Quilting Makes the Quilt*, to demonstrate the importance of choosing a quilting design that will create the desired effect.

OLD ENGLISH TULIPS II,

61" x 63". Stitching in the ditch outlines the tulips in the outer border in this version. A feathered cable defines the cream border. A double feather wreath and a feathered cable add a swirl of curvilinear texture and motion across the center tulips.

OLD ENGLISH TULIPS III,

61" x 63". In a manner derived from English heirloom quilts, this version of Old English Tulips was heavily quilted with feathers, flourishes, and curls done with machine embroidery threads. Notice the use of straight-spine feathers to fill in the edge of the cream border. (This quilt won "Best Machine Quilted" award at the Queensland Quilters Inc. Exhibition, 2001.)

OLD ENGLISH TULIPS IV,

61" x 63". Feathers flow from hearts in the corners of the border that surrounds the center tulip blocks. The tulips sit in a bed of continuous leaf quilting, which flattens and texturizes their background. Stitch-in-the-ditch quilting outlines each flower.

OLD ENGLISH TULIPS V,

77½" x 77½". A cream border surrounds the outer tulips in this variation. Open-feather wreaths are quilted in the tulip blocks, and four separate open-feather corners flow out along the borders. Variegated cotton thread further defines the quilting designs and makes the wreaths more visible on the pieced tulips.

FOREVER AMISH,

90" x 92". I first saw the design for this quilt in the "Lit from Within" Amish Quilt Exhibition sent to Australia. The use of color delighted me and I have remained faithful to the original quilt in my color choices. It is elaborately quilted with feathered designs, far different from the simplistic quilting used in the original. The quilting is more obvious because I chose a thread of deep blue for more contrast. "Forever Amish" won the award for "Best Machine Quilting" at the Queensland Quilters Inc. Exhibition in 1999.

ROMANCE, 2001,

46" x 46". An original whole-cloth quilt filled with feathered hearts— what could be more romantic? Feathered swags encircle the central design. I used a fine, 100-denier silk thread. This quilt won the award for "Best Small Traditional Quilt (professional)" at the Sydney Quilters' Guild Inc. Exhibition in 2002.

WHITE TABLE RUNNER, *16" x 39½".*

The feathered quilting designs in this beautifully textured table runner were specially drawn to fit each shape.
The interior heart perfectly suits the shape of the diamond square pattern set on point in the center of the runner.

APRICOT TABLE RUNNER *16" x 37"*

Beautiful quilting turns an ordinary table runner into one of exquisite texture and beauty. This one
features a simple, double-curved feather chain in the center surrounded by a border of feathered swirls.

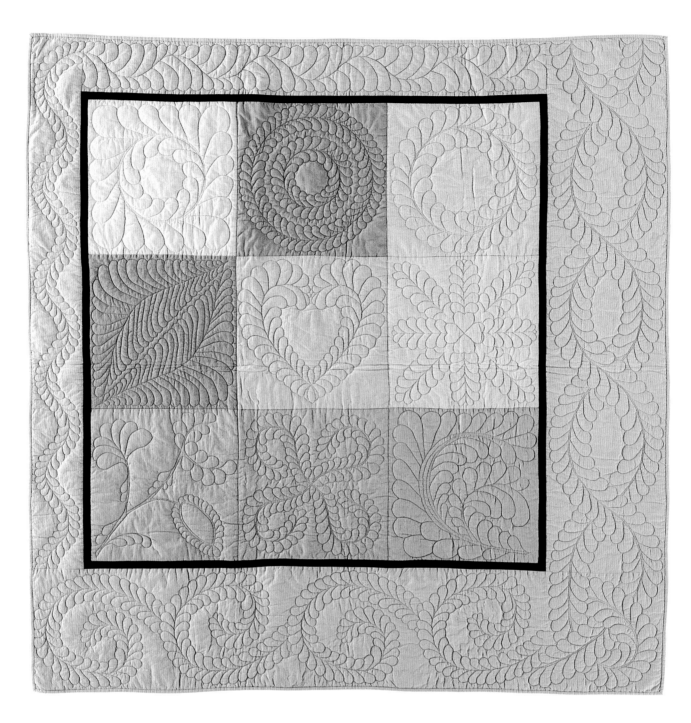

FEATHERED SAMPLER, *59" x 59".*

Notice the different border widths and designs in this quilt—a sampler made to showcase numerous designs for my workshop on creating feathered quilting designs.

LARGE AMISH BARS QUILT, *65" x 65". This quilt is similar to the smaller Amish Bars quilts on pages 63 and 68. The center panel features exactly the same feathered designs. Two additional borders surround the center panel and have the same repeat length for the outer, feathered cable design that was used in the smaller quilts. A straight-spine feather design was quilted along the inner and outer edges of the cable.*

WHOOPSIE HEART, *13½" x 14". This small, whole-cloth wall hanging features double-line machine quilting with metallic thread. The stylized feathered heart in the center is surrounded by stipple quilting and a deep-curve feathered border. The border corners turn on the inside— a variation of the design shown on page 98.*

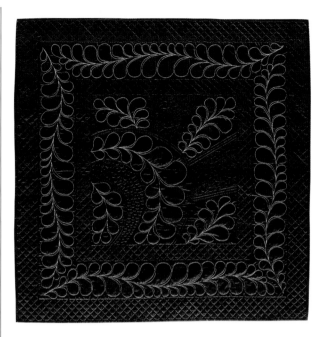

WHITE FEATHERS, *38" x 38". White quilting in heavy cotton thread on black is not the normal choice, but the results are distinctive. It takes practice to machine quilt beautiful, flowing feathers on a dark fabric, because every stitch shows.*

WHITE FEATHERS TOO, *38" x 38". Regular dressmaking thread was used to quilt fast and free feathers on this white-on-white wall hanging. Notice how different they look from the other two White Feather quilts on this page.*

WHITE FEATHERS, VARIEGATED, *2001, 38" x 38". This quilting was done with 30-weight variegated thread. Notice how much more distinctive the feathers are in comparison to those in "White Feathers Too."*

BLUE OPEN FEATHERS, *68" x 35". Feathered hearts and a wreath in the center of this runner are framed with a quilted grid "sashing." The continuous, open-feather curve that surrounds the center is enhanced with additional feathers that fill the open space in the curve. Variegated quilting thread makes the design more pronounced.*

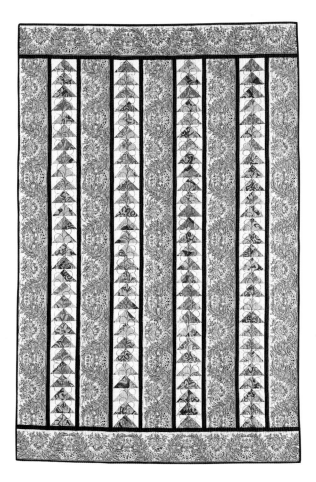

FLYING GEESE, *53½" x 81½". Fast and free feathers flow over the flying geese panels in this colorful strip quilt. The border-print stripes that alternate with the pieced panels are quilted in an adaptation of the same pattern. The feathers were not drawn on the quilt surface but were created as I stitched with variegated cotton thread. This was a suitable method because the strips are quite complex and more traditional feathered designs would haven been difficult to mark and would have been lost in the busy piecing and print patterns.*

CHAPTER 10

General directions

This chapter includes information you will need to transfer your quilting designs to your quilt top and then machine quilt it. A brief review of free-motion machine quilting follows, along with specific directions for quilting feathers. Directions for binding your quilt and for making a hanging sleeve are also included.

Transferring Quilting Designs

The most important thing to consider when transferring a quilting design to the fabric is your choice of marker. Test your marking tool before you use it to mark the pattern on the entire quilt top. Make sure that you can remove all marks easily after you have completed the quilting.

Using a Light Box

Because I draw my quilting designs onto tracing paper, I prefer to use a light box when transferring them onto the quilt top. If you don't own a light box, you can improvise with a glass-topped table or a box topped with a sheet of safety glass or heavy, clear acrylic (perspex in Australia). An extension table with the leaf removed and a piece of safety glass on top is another option. Whichever you choose, place a table lamp beneath it and you're ready to transfer your design.

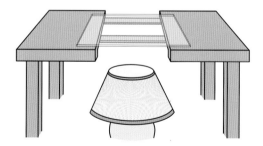

1. Tape the quilting design face up on the glass surface and smooth the quilt top in position over the design.

2. Turn on the light and trace the design onto the quilt top with your marking pen or pencil.

Other Options

If you do not want to use the light-box method, consider the following marking methods and choose one that appeals to you and your working style:

- Layer the quilt top with batting and backing. Pin the design in place on top and do the quilting through the paper. The advantage to this method is obvious—there won't be any marks to remove from the finished project. The disadvantage? You cannot see the fabric while you stitch so you won't be able to see if there are any puckers or wrinkles developing during the actual quilting. In addition, you must have a paper design for every section of the quilt because you will tear away the pattern after you have quilted. As a result, preparation is more time-consuming, but you will get lots of practice drawing feathers!

- Trace the design onto netting (bridal tulle) and then position the netting over the quilt top. Draw the design through the netting onto the quilt top. It is much easier and faster to use bridal tulle than to use a stencil, particularly with all the lines in a feather design. It is permanent and reusable. Because you can see through it, it is also easy to position designs correctly. However, take care with your choice of markers. You should use a permanent marker to draw the design onto the net. If you use a different kind of chemical marker (blue wash-out marker for example) to draw through the net onto your quilt top, the two inks might react together and move the permanent ink off the tulle and onto your quilt top—something you definitely don't want! Be sure to test first!

- Make a design stencil of cardboard or plastic. Place on top of the quilt top and mark along the lines. Personally, I find this to be a labor-intensive method because there are so many lines to transfer in a feathered pattern. The advantage, of course, is that you will have a sturdy, reusable stencil to use again in other projects.

- When the quilt top has busy prints or fabrics that are difficult to mark, I use a combination of methods to mark quilting designs. Pin baste the quilt layers together as usual and quilt in all the seam lines first (stitch in the ditch) to define the areas of the quilt. Choose a backing fabric that is a solid color or a calm, light-colored print so that you can see the markings. After you complete the straight-line, in-the-ditch quilting lines, flip the quilt over and pin baste the layers together from the backing side. Then remove the pin basting from the right side of the quilt layers. Use the in-the-ditch stitching as your guide to position the quilting pattern. Transfer the design to the back of the quilt using the netting method described above. Do the machine quilting from the backing side. Be sure to check your thread tension. You may need to tighten the upper tension a bit in order to draw the bobbin thread into the quilt layers

for an attractive quilting stitch. The bobbin thread will show on the right side of the quilt.

- Do free-form feather quilting on the quilt layers. Lucky you, if you are so gifted! This is where you create the design in your head and quilt directly onto the quilt—no drawing. This may be good for contemporary quilts, but for traditional quilts I find it best to draw the design directly on the quilt top to achieve any degree of accuracy and design uniformity. It's the only way to work out border designs and corners for a perfect fit.

Free-Motion Machine Quilting

What follows is a quick review. For more detailed instructions, check out one of the many good books on machine quilting.

Adjusting the Machine

If you can drop the feed dogs or disengage or cover them in some way, you can do free-motion quilting on your machine. Attach a darning foot or specially designed free-motion embroidery foot. This type of presser foot usually has a spring that puts a little bounce into the stitching motion. Be sure to read your instruction manual before you set up your machine for this technique. On some machines, you may be directed to adjust the pressure on the foot for free-motion quilting or embroidery. (This is *not* the

---

TRANSFERRING BORDER REPEATS

When positioning repeat designs on borders, make a small mark on the quilt top where each repeat should finish. For design-centering purposes, draw a lengthwise line on the actual quilt top along the center of the border design area.

Positioning Marks for Border Repeats

tension knob; many machines do not have a pressure adjustment knob; they are self-adjusting.)

NOTE: Some manuals suggest using a bare needle with no darning foot for free-motion stitching. *Do not follow this recommendation.* It will create more stitching problems than you want, and it's dangerous. It's just too easy to sew through your finger when there is no presser foot to keep your fingers safe!

Choosing a Quilting Thread for Feathered Designs

I never use hand quilting thread in the sewing machine. Traditional feathers that require "double-line" quilting look their best when stitched with dressmaking thread in a color that matches the quilt-top fabric. Monofilament thread is also acceptable. The double line of stitching on the feathers and any wobbles will show less with these choices. I use a size 80 needle for all machine quilting, unless I am using the specialty threads discussed below.

For finely detailed feathers stitched on silk or silk-like fabrics, consider a 100-denier silk thread and a size 60 Sharp or universal needle. Test first on a sample quilt sandwich with the fabrics you are using.

Open feathers and quick-and-easy feathers are outstanding when quilted with heavier threads (30 weight and 40 weight) as well as variegated colors, because they have only a single line of stitching. Use a size 90 topstitching needle with thicker threads to keep them from shredding in the eye of the needle. A size 90 or larger Sharp needle is another option.

Never use a ballpoint needle for any machine quilting. A ballpoint needle is designed for sewing stretch fabrics; it separates the fibers so it can slide between them without snagging the fabric. For quilting, the needle must be one designed to stab through the fabric and the batting for a clean, crisp stitch.

Always test your needle and thread combination first on a sample quilt sandwich with the fabrics you are using and adjust the tension correctly.

A caution is in order here. When you choose thicker threads or contrasting colors for quilting, your quilting errors will be more obvious. In addition, the thicker threads build up faster if you pause too long while the machine is still running; this can make a mess! If you're a beginner, save these specialty threads for the projects you will do after you've gained some skill at free-motion quilting.

My best advice about thread is to be kind to yourself while you are learning. Choose a fine, matching-color thread—and don't look too closely at your first stitched sample. View your work from a distance of two feet to get the overall effect and avoid being overcritical of your efforts. Don't get me wrong; I'm not giving you permission to do sloppy quilting. I am encouraging to give yourself a chance to practice and perfect your free-motion quilting technique. The "quilt police" are not out to get you!

Stitching the Design

With free-motion machine quilting, you are in complete control of where the stitches go and how long they are. The presser foot *does not* exert pressure on the fabric except when picking up the bobbin thread and the feed dogs *do not* work, so you can move the fabric freely underneath the darning foot. If you have never done free-motion stitching, it's a good idea to practice first (see "Note" on page 139).

1. With the quilt under the machine needle, bring the bobbin thread to the top of the quilt.

2. Place your hands on the quilt to create a horseshoe shape around the needle. The fingers and thumbs of both hands should not be touching. Avoid putting your elbows on the table. The motion must come from your shoulders.

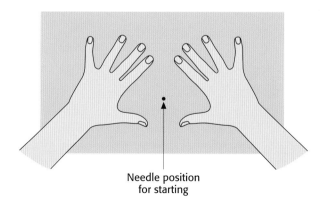

Needle position
for starting

3. Grasp the top and bobbin threads in one hand and start the machine. Use the half-speed setting if available on your machine and put your foot down hard on the pedal. Otherwise, use a medium speed. If you stitch too slowly, the resulting free-motion stitching will be jerky. If you stitch too fast, you lose control of the work. Use your hands to move the quilt and create the stitches at the same time. Remember the feed dogs are not working for you. You must move the fabric away from you to make a line of stitches and then toward you or to the side, depending on the direction you want to stitch. Do not try to use the reverse button when doing free-motion quilting. It won't work.

4. When you begin to stitch, move the fabric only slightly so that the first stitches you take are very tiny—about 6 or 7 stitches over a length of ¼". This will lock your stitches so that you can clip the threads close to the quilt surface rather than backstitch (not attractive) or pull the threads to the underside to tie off. Some machines have an automatic lock-off stitch. Using this feature can result in a knot of thread that looks untidy and often comes undone.

5. As you stitch, strive to make stitches that are similar in length to the stitching length you would normally use when sewing with a regular presser foot and the feed dogs engaged, i.e., 10 to 12 stitches per inch or a stitch length setting of 2 to 2½. When you find a comfortable speed (medium to medium fast), keep it steady in order to keep your stitches as even as possible. With the foot-pedal speed constant, you can concentrate on moving the quilt under the needle and developing a smooth stitching rhythm.

6. Without actually turning it, move the quilt in any direction required to follow the quilting design. Because the feed dogs are disengaged, you can move your work to the left or right, back or forth, and at any angle. If you move your hands in a circle, you will stitch a circle without ever turning the entire quilt in a circle.

7. End a line of free-motion stitching in the same way you started, by taking the last 6 or 7 stitches within the last ¼" of the line you are following.

NOTE: If you have never done any free-motion quilting, it's a good idea to practice first on a quilt sandwich similar to the one you wish to quilt. Do about ten side-by-side lines of stitching on your practice piece, moving the fabric about 2" to 3" for each "push" or "pull" of the quilt sandwich before stopping. Then move your hands so that you can do another ten lines beside the first; then stop again. With a little practice, you will soon discover a comfortable stitching speed and develop a sense of how to move the fabric under the needle in the desired direction.

Free-motion machine stitching makes it easy to follow a complex quilting design without turning the quilt under the needle. It does require developing a measure of control with your hands to create fluid movements, but if you maintain an even, medium to medium-fast speed, this comes more easily. If your stitches are too tiny, your speed is too fast or your hand movements may be too slow. Stitches that are too large indicate that your speed is too slow or your hand movements are too fast. To correct your method, strive to get the foot-pedal speed right first, and then concentrate on your hand movements to get the stitch length you want.

Stop the machine to move your hands into a new position whenever necessary. I stop often to adjust my hand position. This gives me more control and the opportunity to look to see where I should be stitching next. It will also help keep your arms and shoulders relaxed. Do remember to breathe; people often forget.

The sewing machine is a very powerful tool. Take great care to keep your fingers out of the way of the needle while you sew. The consequences of catching your fingernail or your finger can be quite dramatic and costly, requiring a trip to the doctor. On top of the pain, you're likely to get blood on your beautiful quilt!

To stay relaxed while you machine quilt, listen to classical or mood music—nothing too jerky or too loud. It can make a difference in the results!

Machine Quilting Feathers

Most traditional feathers are quilted as directed below, with the exceptions noted. My best advice for learning to stitch any feathered design is to relax, take one feather at a time, and of course, practice, practice, practice! Following are a few basic rules and the step-by-step directions for teaching yourself to machine quilt feathered designs.

Always quilt the spine of the feathers first, *if* they have a spine. Open-feather designs do not. And there may be other exceptions to this rule.

Quilt in the same manner that you drew the feathers—as a half heart. Begin with the same feather that you would if you were beginning to draw your feathered design.

1. Bring the bobbin thread to the top of the quilt where the feather begins—at the beginning of the curve of the half heart.

2. Hold both threads, start the machine, and move the quilt slowly to make 6 or 7 tiny stitches in the first ¼" to begin and lock the threads.

3. In one smooth motion, machine quilt from the starting-point feather down to the spine. Without stopping at the spine, stitch back on top of the stitching you just completed, ending at the starting point for the next feather. I call this technique "double-line quilting."

4. Pause with the needle in the quilt, breathe, and reposition your hands so that you can complete the next feather without stopping partway. Before you begin to stitch, look at the path you will follow to stitch the next feather. Stitch in one smooth motion from the beginning of the new feather to the spine and back again to the beginning of the next feather. Repeat this process until you have completed all the feathers in your design on one side of the spine.

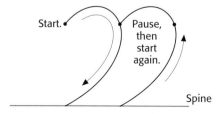

When you are quilting very small feather designs that are only ¼" to ½" high, I recommend quilting as many as possible within your hand span. Then stop the machine before moving your hands.

Stitching in this manner, one feather at a time, is the easiest way to learn to stitch smoothly for accurately quilted feathers. This kind of repetition helps train your eyes and hands to work together to develop your own machine quilting rhythm.

5. If your quilting design includes a heart and/or a teardrop as a turning point along the spine, quilt the spine first (this is always the first step), but include the heart and/or the teardrop as you quilt the spine. Then return to the heart or teardrop to begin quilting the feathers on both sides of the spine; all the feathers start from these turning points. Quilt the feathers as directed in steps 3 and 4 above.

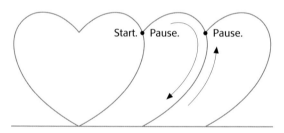

Quilting Long, Thin Feathers

Smooth, wobble-free, double-line quilting is challenging with long, thin feathers. You will need to use a different quilting method for stitching these slender beauties. The size or width of the top of the feather is very small compared to the length of the feather from the spine to the height line—where you would normally do double-line quilting. You will need to stop to reposition your hands at least twice to stitch a long thin feather because of the added length. Referring to the illustration, quilt this type of feather in the following manner:

1. Quilt the spine first.

NOTE: If there are traditional feathers (feathers that have the starting and finishing points in line and perpendicular to the spine line, with double-line quilting on the curve between the height and the spine), quilt them as described in steps 3 and 4 above when you get to them. Most designs with long, thin feathers also have small traditional feathers at the beginning and end of the design.

2. When you quilt the long, thin feathers, stitch the first feather around the curve and down to the spine.

3. Stitch along the spine line (double-line quilting) to the bottom of the second feather. Pause.

4. Stitch up the second feather and around the curve to touch the first feather. Without stopping, stitch back across this line on top of the second feather (double-line quilting) and pause before you start the third feather.

5. Stitch the third feather from the top around the curve, down to the spine, and along the spine a second time to the bottom of the fourth feather.

6. Pause, and then stitch up the fourth feather and around the curve to touch the third feather and back across this line on top of the fourth feather to the fifth feather. Pause.

7. Continue stitching feathers in this manner, with every second feather having double-line quilting along the spine and across the top of the same feather. Use this stitching method until the design is complete or the long, thin feathers become traditional feathers once more.

NOTE: By doing the double-line quilting on the shortest areas of the long, thin feathers, you are less likely to have wobbly quilting lines than if you tried to quilt twice along the long curve between the height line and the spine.

When long, thin feathers are in a corner, try to avoid stitching the double-line quilting on the top of the corner feather, as it tends to be more noticeable. See "Drawing Long Feathers to Fill a Triangle" on page 85. You will need to think ahead and count back from the corner feather to find where you should start in order to avoid doing double-line quilting on the top curve of this feather.

When quilting deep repeat curves (page 93), you must plan ahead so that the last long, thin feather that appears to run into the spine line doesn't have double-line quilting across the top curve and therefore along the long curve of the spine.

Quilting Open Feathers

Open feathers do not require any double-line quilting. I recommend quilting them one at a time to keep the stitching fluid and smooth. Start at a feather where the line changes direction—where the spine line would be if there were one—at a sharp point. Quilt completely around the single feather until the next change of direction or sharp point where the next feather begins. Pause, breathe, move your hands, look where you're going next, and then quilt the next open feather.

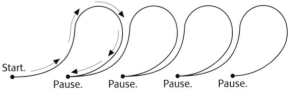

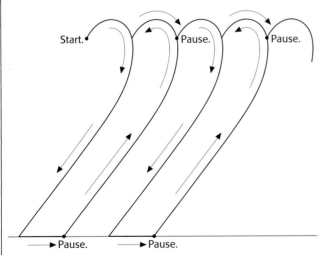

Binding Your Quilt

Cut strips for double-fold binding as specified in the individual quilt directions. Do not trim the backing and batting until after you have attached the binding. All seam allowances are ¼" wide.

1. Sew the cut strips together at a 45° angle and press the seams open.

2. Fold the strip in half lengthwise, wrong sides together, and press.

3. Beginning about 10" from an upper corner, pin the binding to the quilt (or pillow cover) front, leaving a 6"-long tail. Align the raw edges of the binding with the raw edge of the quilt top or the binding positioning line drawn on the quilt top.

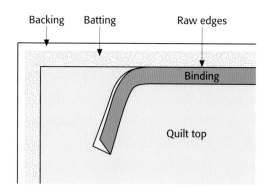

4. Using an even-feed foot, if available, stitch the binding to the quilt. Backstitch at the beginning to secure. Be careful not to stretch the binding as you go. At the corner, stop the stitching ¼" from the edge; backstitch, and clip the threads.

5. Turn the quilt. Fold the binding straight up and away from the quilt to form a 45° angle. Place a straight pin in the binding in line with raw edges of the first side.

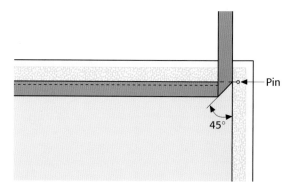

6. Bring the binding straight down over the pin and hold firmly in place while you align the fold in the binding with raw edge of the first side. Make sure the raw edges of the binding are aligned with the raw edge of the second side. Stitch from the top of the fold down the second side, finishing ¼" from the edge.

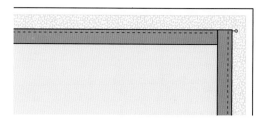

7. Continue sewing and mitering corners on the remaining edges. Finish stitching approximately 6"–8" from the starting point; backstitch and clip the threads.

8. Open the binding and lay one end on top of the other. Trim both ends at a 45° angle, allowing a ½" overlap for seaming. With right sides together, pin and stitch the ends together. Finger-press the seam open.

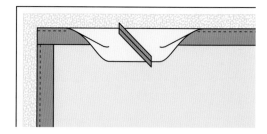

9. Refold the binding and finish stitching to the quilt.

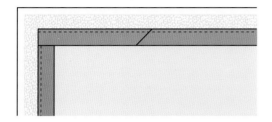

10. Trim the batting and backing even with the raw edges of the binding. If you are planning to add a hanging sleeve, do so now, before sewing the binding to the back. See "Adding a Hanging Sleeve" below.

11. Fold the binding to the back of the quilt and cover the machine stitching with the folded edge. A perfect miter will form on the front of the quilt at each corner. Fold the miter on the back of the quilt in the opposite direction to distribute the bulk evenly. Blindstitch the folded edge of the binding to the quilt, making sure the stitches don't show on the front or back of the quilt. Stitch the miters closed on both sides of the quilt.

Adding a Hanging Sleeve

A sleeve at the top of the backing makes it easy to hang your quilt. For the quilts in this book, the hanging sleeve is most often cut from the backing fabric.

1. Cut a strip of fabric 8" wide and as long as the top edge of the quilt. Turn under and press ½" at each short end. Turn under an additional ½", press, and stitch close to the inner folded edge at each end of the strip.

2. Fold the strip in half lengthwise with wrong sides together. Shift one long edge ¼" below the other, making one side of the sleeve narrower. Press the fold.

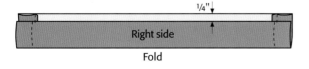

Right side

Fold

3. Mark the center of the rod sleeve and the center of the quilt. With the narrower side of the sleeve against the quilt backing, pin the rod sleeve to the top edge of the quilt, matching centers and aligning all 3 raw edges. The sleeve will "pouf" a bit because the side on top is ¼" larger than the side against the quilt.

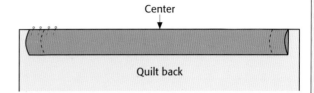

Center

Quilt back

4. Using a ¼"-wide seam allowance, stitch the rod sleeve to the top edge of the quilt, through all thicknesses.

5. Keeping the fabric tube you've created open at both short ends, hand stitch the short ends to the quilt backing. Hand stitch the pressed fold to the quilt, making sure the stitches don't show on the front of the quilt. The extra ¼" of fabric in tube will prevent the rod from distorting the quilt when you hang it.

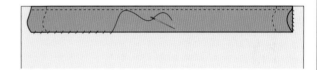

Adding a Label

Be sure to add a cloth label to the back of your finished quilt. Include your name, location, and date. If you have named the quilt, add that to the label along with any other pertinent information about the quilt that you care to include.

About the author

Lee Cleland is a highly regarded freelance quilting teacher and award-winning quiltmaker who delights in using the sewing machine for intricate quilting. She loves sharing these skills with her students, traveling widely throughout Australia, New Zealand, and the United States to do so.

A regular contributor to Australian patchwork magazines, Lee actually made her first quilt in 1968. It was hand appliquéd but machine quilted!

Lee's first book, *Quilting Makes the Quilt,* was published by Martingale & Company. Lee believes that "all quilts should be quilted to death." Her quilts are proof enough of that, as they continue to win major awards at significant Australian quilting shows.

Not too long ago, Lee left Big Smoke (Sydney, Australia) and now lives in the small coastal town of Yamba in northern New South Wales, Australia. She loves it there because of the simple things: she can go barefoot nine months of the year and walk the beach to watch the sun rise each morning when she is home and not traveling to teach somewhere.